Literature
and the Reader:

Research in Response to Literature,
Reading Interests, and the Teaching of Literature

Alan C. Purves
Richard Beach

Literature
and the Reader:
Research in Response to Literature,
Reading Interests, and the Teaching of Literature

Alan C. Purves
Richard Beach

University of Illinois at Urbana-Champaign

Final report to The National Endowment for the Humanities
Project Number H69-0-129
September 1969 - January 31, 1972
24, 210.00

CONSULTANT READERS FOR THIS MANUSCRIPT: Richard Braddock, University of Iowa/G. Robert Carlsen, University of Iowa/Thomas C. Pollock, New York University/Louise M. Rosenblatt, New York University/James R. Squire, Ginn and Company

NCTE COMMITTEE ON PUBLICATIONS Robert F. Hogan, NCTE Executive Secretary, Chairman/Blyden Jackson, University of North Carolina at Chapel Hill/Robert E. Palazzi, Burlingame High School, Burlingame, California/Bette J. Peltola, University of Wisconsin, Milwaukee/Paul O'Dea, NCTE Director of Publications/**EDITORIAL SERVICES** Linda Jeanne Reed, NCTE Headquarters/ **BOOK DESIGN** Kirk George Panikis, NCTE Headquarters

Library of Congress Catalog Card Number LC 72-89632
ISBN 0-8141-2969-2
NCTE Stock Number 29692

Third Printing, August 1976

Contents

Foreword

The undertaking of any review of research is a labor of necessity turned a labor of anxiety. We[1] undertook this study because we felt a need to take stock—we were interested in research in the teaching of literature, yet we realized how little we knew of what we imagined must be the myriad of studies. How many times was old ground retrod? How many good instruments were lying unused? What could we learn about research design?

When we began this review, we faced two major problems: first, finding some way of classifying the studies we were examining; second, dealing with the relationship between the substantive and statistical merits of the studies. Both problems were solved by a combination of planning and history.

We undertook the review in three stages. The first was the delimitation of the areas that we would cover. After assembling an advisory group consisting of A. Lynn Altenbernd, Richard Braddock, G. Robert Carlsen, Paul B. Diederich, Alfred H. Grommon, Charlotte S. Huck, Helen Lodge, James E. Miller, Jr., Bernard O'Donnell, Paul Olson, Thomas C. Pollock, Louise Rosenblatt, Henry Sams, and James R. Squire, we asked them to review a preliminary sketch of those areas and a first-order bibliography. At a meeting of the entire group, we decided that we would remain somewhat confined, that we would consider literature as the written word, and that we would consider it only in its aesthetic and humanistic aspects. We also decided that we would not consider film or the process of read-

---

1. The initial investigators were Alan L. Madsen and Alan C. Purves. After the bibliographic stage, Richard Beach replaced Alan Madsen.

ing or learning to read. We would review studies at all grade levels, and we would not exclude studies that were not empirical or experimental—this meant that we would look at case studies, although we agreed that a critic's writing would not be considered a case study.

During and after the meeting with our advisory board, we met with resistance to many of our a priori formulations—we had developed a classificatory scheme and a rigorous review procedure before the session. The committee argued—with justice, we thought —that the classification of the studies would have to fall out of the examination of them. Members also argued that nearly any study could be faulted on some technicality. For instance, nearly all of the studies of the effects of literature on attitudes fail to consider the work read as one of hundreds of independent variables influencing an attitude. Nearly all the studies that use factor analysis overlook the objections to the technique. Nearly all correlational studies are simplistic; nearly all treatment studies overshorten the length of treatment or fail to dichotomize the experimental variables sufficiently, so that no significant differences appear. What is more important than these criticisms, which have been made over and over, is to determine what these studies have hinted at and pointed to and what strategies might be employed in future research.

We have emerged, therefore, with a fairly rough classification of studies: studies of the nature of responses to literature and how they might be measured; studies of reading preferences (the largest number of studies of any single type); and studies of classroom treatment, including summative evaluations of curricula. The first two types of studies form the largest portion of the studies we have covered. In reading through them we have derived subcategories as well, as the various chapters will show. In making these categorizations, we acknowledge their nontaxonomic character and their interrelatedness. They have proved useful to us and we hope will not prove too unwieldy or too unfamiliar to the reader.

The second stage of the review was to enlarge our bibliography, which we did by a literature search and an appeal to the members

of the NCTE Conference on English Education, the National
Conference on Research in English, the readership of *Research in
the Teaching of English*, an NCTE journal, and the directors of
English education at several research institutions. From this cul-
ling, we amassed a list of over 1200 items, all of which had to be
reviewed. Many were eliminated because they did not deal with the
topic or were not reports of research. The bibliographies at the ends
of the chapters include those studies which were found to be appropriate. Although our original cutoff date was 1969, we have included
studies published as recently as June 1971. Where possible, we
looked at the works themselves; in many instances, however, we
relied on outside reviewers, and we are grateful for the help of
Anthony Amato, Floyd Bergman, Earl Buxton, John B. Carroll,
John Connor, Charles Cooper, Kenneth Donelson, Margaret Early,
Edward Fagan, Donald Gallo, Oscar Haugh, George Hillocks, Jr.,
Ted Hipple, William J. Hoetker, William Hoth, Lois S. Josephs,
Stephen Judy, Herbert Karl, Pose Lamb, Mitchell Leaska, Geral-
dine LaRocque, Stoddard Malarkey, Augustine McPhail, Ben F.
Nelms, Douglas Nietzke, Norine Odland, Walter Petty, Geneva
Pilgrim, Paul Schied, Anthony Tovatt, L. Ramon Veal, Donald
Vieth, Joel Weiss, Leonard Woolf, and Frank Zidonis.

After we had read the works, there came the far more compli-
cated and more time-consuming task of digesting them. In the
writing which follows, we have described the research design only
when we found it germane to the study; our attention is on what
has been studied and what has been discovered.

In considering the value of each study, we have tended to look
at the importance of the question with which it deals and at the
conceptualization of the design more than at the statistical treatment used. We have done so because many worthwhile studies
used techniques which have since been superseded, yet the studies
were powerful in the ways in which they conceived of the problem.
I. A. Richards' *Practical Criticism* is the master study of a whole
group, yet as a content analysis it is highly subjective and selective.

As Conrad put it, "What redeems it is the idea." Many other studies, equally important, use the case study or the introspective technique. Their findings are often more convincing than are large-scale studies, even though there are difficulties in generalizing from them.

In deciding that we would look at the questions raised and the logic of the study rather than at its purely statistical properties, we did not neglect the logic of the statistical design. Many studies, however well conceived, foundered because inappropriate statistical procedures were used. Correlation and analysis of variance were the most frequent treatments employed; they were often inappropriate to the questions asked in the study or raised in the data. At times there was a need for multiple analysis of variance, as in the Coryell study, for discriminant function analysis, or for some other technique. Often, of course, these techniques did not exist when the study was conducted, and we have tried to avoid the smirking of hindsight.

In addition to the advisory committee and the reviewers, there are several people that we must acknowledge: Herbert MacArthur of the National Endowment for the Humanities; James Wardrop, our statistical referee; Gunnar Hansson of Göteborg University; Sharon Walsh, our research assistant; Doris Hill, Jenny Quillinan, and Bonita Higgerson, our typists; and the entire reference department of the University of Illinois library.

Our thanks, too, to the hundreds of researchers and their subjects. They have all labored mightily. We think that their labor was not in vain.

Studies of
Response to Literature

The studies of response to literature may be divided in a number of ways, to be sure, and each division is an unclear classification, both because many studies can fall into two categories and because the process of response is itself not easily divisible. Nonetheless, we have arrived at the following general headings:

> Studies of the factors in understanding
> Studies of the factors in rating or judging
> Studies of the factors of stated responses
> Studies of preconceptions and their effect on response
> Studies of the process of response
> Studies in general effects of literature
> Studies in bibliotherapy
> Studies of the factors in literary learning
> Development of literature tests

A. Studies of the Factors in Understanding

The major study here, to which all others must be related, is I. A. Richards' *Practical Criticism* (1929), which is a large-scale case study of the written responses of university students to thirteen poems. Richards logically and empirically isolated ten factors which appeared to hamper "correct" understanding and judgment:

1. failure to make out the plain sense or to understand poetry "as a set of ordinary intelligible English sentences";

2. difficulties in sensuous apprehension of the rhythm of words and phrases;

3. difficulties in visualizing imagery;
4. mnemonic irrelevancies which lead readers to digress;
5. stock responses to the content of works;
6. oversentimentality in response;
7. overinhibition in response;
8. doctrinal adhesions about the world which interfere in reading;
9. technical presuppositions about how literary writing should be done;
10. general critical preconceptions about literature.

Rosenblatt (1938, 1968) added to Richards' concentration on analyses of readers' comments an emphasis both on the process by which what the reader brings to the text interacts with its special character to result in his interpretation, and on the teaching process. This provided the theoretical frameworks or hypotheses for a number of the studies of response, bibliotherapy, and teaching methods.

Richards' categories have been explicitly tested in only three studies: Glicksberg (1944) found them to be appropriate to an analysis of fifteen students at Harvard; Livingston (1968) replicated the study with graduate teachers and high school students and found all groups equally inadequate; and Hansson (1959) corroborated the findings with Swedish students. Other studies have brought their own classification systems (Irion, 1925; Pickford, 1935; Davis, 1944; Harris, 1948; Black, 1954; Carroll, 1960; Squire, 1964; Dill and Purves, 1967; Ring, 1968) based on examination of student responses or of tests and test items. That these classifications of problems in reading and understanding overlap a great deal might be anticipated and may be generalized as follows:

    I. Insufficient information: lack of background information in general (Irion, Black) or lack of knowledge about the

allusions in the work itself (Black; Dill and Purves);
failure to see context (Black; Dill and Purves); failure to
know literary devices (Davis; Dill and Purves); failure
to apply information (Dill and Purves).

II. Failure to understand or cognitive failure.
   A. Diction: failure to recognize synonyms for uncommon words (Harris); failure to understand difficult words (Black); lack of word knowledge (Irion, Davis); failure to understand words from context (Davis).
      1. Mnemonic problems with words (Pickford, Richards).
      2. Rationalization (Pickford).
   B. Syntax: inability to recognize antecedents in syntactic abnormality (Harris); lack of knowledge of expression (Irion); making out plain sense (Richards).
   C. Imagery and metaphor: inability to deal with obstructive imagery (Pickford); failure to recognize equivalent of figurative language (Richards, Harris); failure to understand metaphor (Black).
   D. Inference about parts: inability to get specifics (Irion); failure to grasp detailed statements (Davis); failure to analyze parts (Dill and Purves).
   E. Inference about the whole theme or idea: failure to recognize summaries of ideas (Harris); difficulty in inferring meaning (Davis), in selecting the main thought (Davis), and in making logical inference (Carroll); inability to see the main point (Irion); puzzlement (Pickford).
   F. Inference about characters: failure to recognize summaries of characters (Harris).
   G. Inference about tone, mood, or intent: failure to recognize authors' attitude (Harris); misunderstanding of or failure to identify intention (Davis, Black);

difficulty in detecting irony (Black); failure to perceive focus (Ring).

H. Inference about structure: inability to relate technique to meaning (Harris); failure to follow organization (Davis); failure to analyze whole (Dill and Purves).

I. Other: inability to make comparisons (Pickford).

III. Psychological problems.

A. Aesthetic distance: failure to defend against emotional disturbance (Pickford); oversentimentality and inhibition (Richards).

B. Preconceptions (Black); egocentric perception (Ring); attitude as set approach, attitude as obstacle (Pickford); doctrinal adhesions, technical presuppositions, critical preconceptions (Richards).

C. Tendency to invent details (Ring); happiness binding, the desire for happy endings (Squire).

D. Dominance of rhythm (Pickford).

E. Feelings: feelings *of* an emotion and feelings *that* such and such will be or is (Pickford); feelings of pleasure and pain (Pickford); stock responses (Richards).

F. Lack of attention or concentration.

As we look at these classes, we can note the high probability of lack of information and lack of vocabulary as anterior conditions to the others (certainly to the others in the cognitive group). One study confirms the primacy of word knowledge (Irion, 1925). A small study sought to probe the relationship between vocabulary and three other factors in literature understanding (discovery of theme, reader participation, and apprehension of sensory images). The study examined sixth graders and found weak correlation between vocabulary and the three factors (the strongest was with apprehension of imagery—.56). Word building ability, on the other hand, was virtually independent. The three factors contained an intercorrelation of .30 (Garrison and Thomas, 1930). This study partially supports that of Weekes (1929), who found figurative language more of a problem than syntax to ten and twelve year olds. The inaccurate interpretation of metaphoric language also affected preference. Burton (1952) found a clear correlation between literary appreciation and intelligence. One other study (Jenkinson, 1957) sought to relate ability as measured by a "cloze" test to other aspects of literary understanding and found that students in grades ten through twelve who performed well on the test were better able to recognize implied meanings, inference, and syntactic clues; to discuss sound and style; and to formulate their ideas. Their understanding of words and word meaning was not greater than that of those of lesser ability. We still have scant information on the interrelation of the various literary abilities, save that the "analytic" and "synthetic" abilities seem to be discrete.

We also have little information on the relationship between the cognitive factors and the psychological ones. Several studies have shown a relationship between interest in the text and understanding of it (Figurel, 1942; Alpert, 1955; Berstein, 1955; Squire, 1964), but few indicate whether one precedes the other or whether their relationship is like that of Yan and Yin. Vine (1970) found that students who understood the texts better also displayed more interest and less varied responses than the less able students on a semantic differential about the poem. One study (Alpert, 1955) does suggest that females who are able to project themselves read better, but he is unsure whether the factor is projection or emotional involvement. If it is the latter, as he suspects, his study confirms Squire's conclusion that those who become involved read with a higher level of comprehension.

Two other factors have been studied: the relation of age and of background to understanding. Older people do seem to be able to understand works better than younger people (Matson, 1953; Burgdorff, 1966, inter al.), but one can challenge this seemingly obvious finding by pointing out that the criterion is the understanding of an adult (the examiner), so that one might expect older children to think more like adults than younger children. Monson (1966) found a relation between socioeconomic group and the kinds of questions students asked—whether structured or unstructured— and Burgdorff investigated socioeconomic class and understanding by testing children in grades four, five, and six on the ability to draw inference from various works. Socioeconomic class had no significant relation to score except with the subgroup that read the selections for themselves. When the reading factor was removed (when other children heard the selections read aloud), the correlation dropped.

Twenty years ago (1953) Loban sought to describe the reader in terms of his social sensitivity. Finding high school students who ranked at the extremes of two scales of social sensitivity, he gathered their written responses to ten short stories, designed to evoke sympathetic responses, and to certain structured questions. There were significant (.01) differences between the two groups. In addition, the following inferences were drawn: the least sensitive readers wanted to project the blame for a social ill on others; the most sensitive had the most to say. In general, both groups tended to miss thematic implications, to remain superficial, to be unsure of what they wanted to say, to receive new concepts or values cooly, and to reject characters who seemed out of their emotional range.

A few researchers have sought to probe the differences between "good" and "bad" readers. In 1958 Letton showed that readers in the low-scoring group of two sets of ninth grade students tended to inhibit their oral responses to a poem more and tended to use the exact words of the poem more than those in the high-scoring group. Two groups, however, were similar in their ability to note comparisons, to use illustrations in talking, and to relate their personal experiences to the poem. The low-scoring students also liked poetry less than the others and were able to identify fewer poems and poets on a checklist. Letton's first finding seems to be supported by another study (Swain, 1953), which found that "good" readers, as measured by the USAF tests of General Educational Development, tended to restructure meaning, to reorganize meaning for some purpose, more than did "poor" readers. Monson, dealing with fifth grade students in 1966, found that students in the high ability group judged humorous excerpts as humorous more often than did students in the middle and low groups. Rogers (1965) found that differences between the high and low groups of eleventh graders occur in their comparative familiarity with the short story and with authors, in their ability to grasp literal meaning, and in their ability to grasp implied meaning. Clearly, however, the studies of differences have not sought to explore fully the relationship between performance in one skill and performance in the others in order to get a sharp picture of the development of each skill in reading literary texts and in forming adult understandings of those texts.

B. Studies of the Factors in Rating or Judging

For as long as there have been studies of understanding there have been studies of the rating of literary selections by students. These studies have sought to define the premises of taste, just as Richards' study sought to define the premises of understanding. In another section we shall deal at length with the interests and preferences of students; here we are concerned with the reasons students give for the judgments they make. The studies encompass two major types: those examining the relationship between expert and inexpert judgment and those examining the stated reasons for judgment. The validity of the former studies may generally be questioned for their assumption of the correctness of the expert judgment. The latter may be criticized for their overreliance on factor analysis (a form of statistical manipulation not above suspicion). With this caveat, we may look at the categorizing studies.

Most of the studies first identify a general factor of liking or interest or judgment, a factor which is holistic and partially intuitive (Williams, Winter, and Woods, 1938; Eysenck, 1940-1941; Gunn, 1951; Carroll, 1960, 1968). Other factors can be grouped into formal, content-bound, personal, and miscellaneous categories. This division is not neat, for as one looks at many studies, one notes a blending of form and content and of subject and object. In fact, one series of studies (Carroll, 1960, 1968) purports to be defining the factors of prose style but, under scrutiny, seems more to be defining factors of judgment or taste. Nonetheless we might say that the following factors have been isolated:

I. General liking (Gunn; Williams, Winter, and Woods).
   A. General stylistic—including good, pleasant, strong in form and content (Carroll, 1960, 1968).
   B. Simple/complex in form and content (Eysenck); clear (Harpin); ambiguous and capable of many interpretations (Husband).
   C. Imaginative (Harpin, Husband).

II. Formal factors.
   A. Polished and classical as opposed to abandoned and romantic (Williams, Winter, and Woods; Eysenck); sophisticated (Rees and Pedersen).
   B. Ornamental (Carroll, 1960, 1968).
   C. Rhythmic, musical, rhymed (Gunn); language and rhythm (Feasy).
   D. Suitability of expression (Gunn).
   E. Characterization (Carroll, Feasy).

III. Content factors.
   A. Emotionality or personal appeal (Eysenck, Gunn).
   B. Appeal of subject (Gunn, Feasy).
   C. Imagery (Gunn, Feasy).
   D. Abstractness (Carroll, 1960).

E. Seriousness (Carroll, 1960, 1968).

F. Realism (Harpin).

IV. Personal factors.

    A. Personal affect (Arnold, 1960); personal appeal (Carroll, 1968); subjective judgment (Feasy); emotional appeal (Gunn).

    B. Association (Feasy); familiarity (Rees and Pedersen).

    C. Sympathetic identification (Husband).

    D. Masculinity and extroversion (Rees and Pedersen).

    E. Sophistication or literary socialization (Rees and Pedersen).

V. Miscellaneous.

    A. Author (Feasy).

    B. Pragmatic (the piece is singable) and objective (the piece is short) (Feasy).

We can see that these factors might not be equal in importance, and, indeed, the general factor is the most important in most judgments (Williams, Winter, and Woods; Eysenck; Gunn; Carroll, 1960, 1968). The next most important factor seems to deal with the opposition of form and content (Gunn; Williams, Winter, and Woods; Eysenck) or the personal appeal (Carroll, 1968). There is also a split between the personal (pleasure) and impersonal (beauty) judgments (Valentine, 1960). The other factors account for only a minor portion of the variance in judgment. We might conclude then that research has not probed the premises of taste too deeply. The deepest probe (Carroll, 1960) still reveals how much more can be known about the objective attributes of the work that most influence the judgment of its readers than can be known about the work's style, which cannot be used as a measure to clearly explain taste.

As one goes beyond these factors to an examination of the concomitants and causes of judgment, the issues become even cloudier. Several studies have sought to relate judgment to achievement or intelligence. The results are indeterminate. In one study, the less able students chose the more ambiguous works (Husband, 1945), but this study is complemented by a study which shows that younger students (and presumably less able ones) prefer direct to oblique works (Eppel, 1950). In general, both conclusions are confirmed by a study correlating taste with achievement (Harpin) and with intelligence (Carroll, 1934). Herbert Carroll's Prose Appreciation Test is not satisfactory, and his study seems to be refuted by another using his own measure with retarded and superior readers (Schubert, 1953) and by an earlier study (Rohn and Briggs, 1923), but the evidence is far from conclusive.

Studies that investigate the relationship between age and judgment agree that older students tend to conform more closely to adult judgment (Abbott and Trabue, 1921; Britton, 1954; Harpin, 1966). Britton, in fact, found the factor of complexity related to age and concluded that inexperienced readers reject what they don't understand, a finding later confirmed in studies by Alpert (1955) and Squire (1964). Readers rejected false-simple poems and liked true-simple and false-complex poems. Science students preferred simple and restrained poems, but in general they preferred complex poetry. When students returned to the task, they tended to choose the "true" poems. Abbott and Trabue found that younger children's taste is more erratic than that of older children; younger children tended to prefer the sentimental or the comprehensible to the "true" version of a poem.

Few studies have gone deeply into the psychological backgrounds of taste. One found no relationship between the judgment (based on the Carroll Prose Appreciation Test) and the emotional involvement of eleventh graders, although there was some relationship between reported emotional involvement and interest (Evans, 1968). A second study (Wilson, 1956) found some congruence between preference and ego-ideal types or alien types of characters in the work preferred. In a related area, a third study (Weekes, 1929), examining children aged ten and twelve, found that experience did affect judgment and choice (it is difficult to determine whether this is a study more of interests or of taste). Another study found that task determined choice; students rated poems for discussion by a professor differently from their ratings for discussion with a friend (Kammann, 1966).

On the relationship between literary judgment and judgment in the other arts, there is conflicting evidence. Two studies indicate low correlations between literary judgment and musical judgment (Rigg, 1937) and between literary judgment and judgment of drawing (Speer, 1929). But this evidence is somewhat contradicted by the work of Valentine (1962), who has found a general aesthetic factor in his studies, and he tends to corroborate Eysenck (1940-1941). This problem needs to be taken up more fully and with more complex instrumentation (a familiar cry about studies of literary response, as we shall see later here).

One study deserves special attention, because it is among the few that tend to explore the stated reasons for literary preference. In 1969 Ash developed a measure of literary judgment and used it with eleventh grade students. He did find girls significantly superior to boys (corroborating Weekes, 1929, and Carroll, 1930, inter al.), but the significant part of the study came when he interviewed high-, middle-, and low-scoring students to find why they chose the responses they did. Eleven categories were identified: guess, misreading, unsupported judgment, supported judgment, poetic preconception, isolated elements, narrational response, technical response, irrelevant association, interpretation, and self-involvement. The list is heterogeneous and provocative: guess and misreading refer to aspects of understanding; preconception refers to a criterion of taste; irrelevant association, interpretation, and self-involvement refer to aspects of personal involvement; and unsupported judgment, supported judgment, isolated elements, narrational response, and technical response refer to aspects of the process of making judgment as a rhetorical, and perhaps an intellectual, operation. Granted that understanding, criteria, and personal involvement are all constituents of taste, one wonders how they are related to the rhetoric of defending judgment. A further question occurs when one considers the value judgments implicit in some of the categories; perhaps the researcher and the students saw this test not as a measure of inquiry but as a judgmental measure. There were right and wrong answers, as there seem to have been in all the studies referred to in this section. Yet we know that taste is a shifting matter, and even to assume that the author's original version is the standard is a strong assumption. A second problem in this kind of research is that the students are looking for a "right" answer and so do not let the researchers know what their taste is. We single out the Ash study, therefore, because of its value in pointing to needed directions in research and because it demonstrates the pitfalls in this sort of measurement—measurement that ought, certainly, to be pursued.

C. Studies of the Factors of Stated Responses

One of the major research problems concerning response to literature has been that of describing the content of spoken or written responses of individuals or groups. The designations of certain critical schools do not suffice for educational research, and the terms of rhetorical analysis encompass only the form of the stated response. A number of researchers have worked on classificatory systems, always a perilous task because of the arbitrary nature of most schema for content analysis. In other sections we have looked at schemata for judgment and schemata for understanding; now we turn to schemata for the stated response or for criticism.

The major studies working at such classification include those of Meckel (1946), Taba (1955), Squire (1964), Purves and Rippere (1968), and Morris (1969). To these might be added such works as those of critics like Northrop Frye, René Wellek and Austin Warren, Meyer Abrams, and Morris Weitz, who seek to classify schools of criticism, and those of Bloom and Krathwohl, Guilford, and other educational psychologists who seek to classify general verbal or intellectual behavior. But we are primarily concerned with the methods of schematizing nonprofessional responses to literature, which seem to fall into five general groupings:

I. The personal statement: related to pragmatic criticism (Abrams).
   A. Personal psychological (Meckel); self-reference (Taba); associational (Squire, Morris); reader connotative (Skelton).
   B. Reaction to content (Purves and Rippere); prescriptive judgment (Squire); reaction general, awareness of one's own response (Morris); self-involvement (Squire); reaction to literature, reaction to form (Purves and Rippere).

II. Descriptive responses: objective criticism (Abrams); literal criticism (Frye); description (Weitz).
   A. Narrational reaction (Squire); perception of content (Morris; Purves and Rippere); comprehension (Morris); statement of facts (Taba); quotation (Morris); denotative (Skelton).
   B. Perception of language, perception of literary devices, perception of structure, perception of tone, relation of form to content (Purves and Rippere); technical-critical (Meckel); formal criticism (Frye).
   C. Classification by genre, classification by context (Purves and Rippere); descriptive criticism (Frye).

III. Interpretative responses: interpretation (Squire, Purves and Rippere, Weitz, Morris); mimetic criticism (Abrams).
   A. Explanation (Taba); use of experience to explain

behavior (Taba); interpretation of parts (Purves and Rippere).
B. Content-ideational (Meckel); author-connotative (Skelton); generalization from facts (Taba); normative generalizations (Taba); mimetic interpretation, typological interpretation, hortatory interpretation (Purves and Rippere); pragmatic criticism (Abrams); mythical criticism (Frye); anagogic criticism (Frye).

IV. Evaluative responses: evaluation (Taba, Morris, Squire, Purves and Rippere, Weitz).
A. Appreciation (Morris); affective evaluation (Purves and Rippere); like-dislike (Skelton); pragmatic criticism (Abrams).
B. Technical-critical (Meckel); evaluation of method (Purves and Rippere).
C. Evaluation of author's vision (Purves and Rippere); mimetic criticism (Abrams).

V. Miscellaneous responses (Taba, Squire, Morris, Purves and Rippere).
A. Comment about interview (Morris); unrelated-unattempted (Skelton); incomplete verbalization (Morris).
B. Poetics (Weitz).

This meta-description deserves a note or two. The research seems to differentiate between the personal responses that refer to oneself and one's associations and those that refer to one's feelings about the work and one's relation to it. The first is more clearly autobiographical and directed away from the work towards the reader's context, memories, friends, and the like. The second is directed at the work and the reader's feelings about it. Purves and Rippere (1968) fail to note that distinction, preferring the distinction between reaction to form and reaction to content. The division of form and content, other taxonomists agree, applies to description, but perhaps less so to the personal statement. Interpretation is generally divided into specific interpretation, explaining characters, phrases, and other parts of the work, and general interpretation, explaining the whole work. Evaluative statements are usually categorized according to three other groupings: a work is praised or blamed for its evocative power, for its construction, or for its meaningfulness.

In addition to the classification of responses, researchers have tested hypotheses concerning the effects of age and text on critical responses. Scribner (1960), Purves and Rippere (1968), Cooper (1969), and Morris (1969) found that older children devoted much time to interpretation. Fredholm (1970) found that high school readers tended to prefer personal evaluative criteria and teachers tended to prefer formal criteria. Squire (1964) found in a study of 25 boys and 27 girls in the ninth and tenth grades that sex was not a determinant of response—except with certain parts of certain stories—and that intelligence and reading measures do not predict the quality or type of response. He did find that the category of responses were partly determined by the selection, but also by the point in reading the selection at which the response was made. Interpretational responses increased in frequency as students progressed through the stories, and literary judgment and self-involvement responses also increased and were associated with each other. In 1971 Fanselow replicated Squire's study with bilingual students and found they made fewer judgments and interpretations than did Squire's students, pointing, perhaps, to cultural or educational differences between groups. Morris (1969) found that college students appeared to fall into two groups, one dealing with perception and association, one dealing with comprehension and interpretation. Cooper (1969) confirmed Squire's finding about sex and response, and he also found that reading ability is correlated with response choice (better readers choose interpretation; poorer readers, evaluation).

In an earlier study Meckel (1946) had found that of 96 high school seniors 76 percent gave personal psychological responses to a novel, 40.6 percent content-ideational responses, and 34.4 percent technical-critical responses (some gave more than one type of response). This finding must complement Squire's (1964) finding that about 60 percent of student responses to short stories are content-ideational, about 20 percent personal-psychological, and about 15 percent technical-critical (because the categories used by the two are not the same, only a rough comparison can be made). The results of Taba's (1955) study of eighth graders agree more with Squire's than with Meckel's. Cooper (1969), using Purves' categories, found that 39 percent would fall into Meckel's content-ideational category; 18 percent into the personal-psychological category; and 18 percent into the technical-critical category (another 25 percent are inconsistent, so that extrapolation from Cooper's figures would lead to a profile similar to Squire's). There would seem to be two possible explanations of the shift: first, that the curriculum has changed since Meckel's study was undertaken and that the content-ideational or interpretative response has become more prized by teachers and therefore more "popular" with students; second, that the categories of personal-psychological and content-ideational or engagement and interpretation contain overlap—it is often hard to determine whether a stated meaning is personal or "objective." It would seem that for all the researchers the dominant response deals with the content of the work, not its form, and with the work's relation to the reader and his world rather than with the objective or aesthetic qualities of the work.

In a study related to these, Hansson (1964) used the semantic differential, not to assess ratings of poems, but to see what changes in response occurred during the reading of the text. He used 24 scales and had students apply all of them after every second line of a 24-line poem. Three groups participated: university and college teachers of literature, first-year university students in literature, and people with only secondary school education. The three groups were similar in the profiles on each of the dimensions, a finding that differs from Cooper's findings (1969) and from Hansson's earlier study (1959), a replication of Richards' practical criticism study, in which individuals had to formulate their own responses. This pair of studies might indicate that what we consider differences in the ability to respond might well be differences in the ability to express oneself about one's response, and that the response type is less related to intelligence than one might suspect.

D. Studies of Preconceptions and Their Effect on Response

The number of studies of the preconditions of response, either cognitive or attitudinal, are several and fall into clear groups, each of which presents an unsolved problem.

One of the first problems is that of the relationship between interest in the selection and understanding of it. In 1933 Sussams clearly answered that comprehension precedes appreciation. Others are much less sure, asserting that there is a relationship (Figurel, 1942; Alpert, 1955; Bailey, 1955; Berstein, 1955; Shnayer, 1967; Squire, 1964) but it is slight (Groff, 1955). Some claim that perhaps the relationship works the other way. Crossen (1946) found that ninth grade students who were unfavorably disposed toward the content (in this case black) did read the stories less well than those who were neutral. Favorably disposed students did not read better. In a more penetrating study dealing primarily with expository material, McKillop (1957) found that a reader's verbally expressed attitude affected his responses to highly structural factual questions less than it affected questions of judgment and evaluation. From this we might infer that Sussams' initial statement needs to be examined and the definition of *understanding* needs to be made more specific.

Two studies go briefly into home preconditions of response. Both find the home variables important in their relation to the ability to read, and both find that home literary environment is more important than socioeconomic background. It is also an important variable in relation to reading interest, more so than is intelligence, but not, perhaps, in relation to the actual number of books read (Wollner, 1949; Hansen, 1967). Both studies suffer in part from the kinds of measures used, in that interest-in-reading measures are quite easy for students to see through and thus to give what they think is the preferred response. Since both studies deal with younger children (fourth and eighth grades) this cynical interpretation might not be generally applicable, but the question of what the best index of interest in reading literature may be remains.

Aside from interest in reading miscellaneous literary works, we come to the question of what might be the causes of interest in specific works. Why is a work a favorite? Why is it interesting? In general, the answer seems to be that the subject matter is interesting if it is related to the personal experience of the reader (Sussams, 1933; Boyd and Mandler, 1955; Berninghausen and Faunce, 1964; Barrett and Barrett, 1966). People tend to get more involved in that which is related to them, and they tend to seek the work with which they can identify, or the character who resembles them (Loban, 1953; Stout, 1964; Barrett and Barrett). This whole area is more fully covered in chapter 2.

Beyond seeking out familiar characters, people tend to judge most favorably those characters who are most like them (Stout), so that perhaps the author is not entirely in control. In fact, one might go so far as to say that identification easily becomes projection and that readers impute values to characters that are not contained in the story (McCaul, 1944). Downey (1929) had inferred from her data that there are three degrees of self-projection: detached (which may make a visual projection), sympathetic, and empathetic (both of which might be kinesthetic as well as visual). She inferred too that readers often supply their own background to works. Shirley (1966) expanded upon Downey's scale to define seven types: the indifferent, the observer, the partial participator, the intense participator, the self-image synthesizer, the construct synthesizer, and the decision maker. Individual patterns depended in part on the type of work discussed. Kingston and White (1967) found that personality and self-concept variables predicted some of the semantic factors (using the semantic differential) students attributed to the protagonist. The evaluation factor was independent, but potency, activity, and anxiety in the protagonist were seen in terms of the self-concept of the students. Thayer and Pronko probed this phenomenon fully in two related studies (1958, 1959). In the first, students read fictional excerpts that contained no physical description of the characters, yet they reported overwhelmingly that they had a mental picture of the characters and often agreed among themselves about the character. In the second, researchers found that readers will ascribe to liked character traits and attitudes considered likeable, regardless of whether the author portrays those traits. The evidence is less clear concerning the readers' attitudes about the moral issues and the moral positions in the work, but the judgment of characters seemed based less on the abstract moral position of readers than on their attitude toward their friends. All of these studies indicate clearly the importance of projection in the response and understanding of readers, an importance attested to by psychological researchers, both Freudian and non-Freudian (Shrodes, 1949; Loban, 1953; Lesser, 1957; Holland, 1968).

Some research has gone into more detailed aspects of the relationship between personality and response. Grace and Lohmann (1952) investigated second grade children's reactions to stories with child-parent conflicts. The children were in several subgroups (race, socioeconomic status, and whether or not living with both parents). The response most frequently reported was that designated *active opposition* ("It was wrong."), and the least common was the *emotional response* ("It was sad."). The constructive ("They should have.") and the complaint ("I disagree.") were equally frequent. Age and sex made little difference; whites used more active opposition responses than blacks, and children with both parents showed more constructive emotional responses and fewer compliance responses than children with one or none. In a broader study involving older children in Alabama and Connecticut, Stewart found that literary character preferences were related to the personality and culture of the reader, but the nature of the relationship between preference and reader personality variables depends on cultural patterns of acceptance or rejection in the group (Stewart, 1947). The design of this study is weak, but it does indicate a number of sources worth exploring, perhaps in the way that Grace and Lohmann explored them.

Finally, there should be mention of two studies (Michael, Rosenthal, and DeCamp, 1949; Philip, 1951) which disagree on whether the author's name affects students' rating of literary selections. Philip finds it does; the second study finds that neither the prestige of the writer nor the students' knowledge of the definition of the type of selection is a major determinant of the rating of a selection.

There is fairly good evidence, then, that the interest and preconceptions of the reader are important ingredients in literary response, preference, and understanding, and it seems clear that this phenomenon is fairly constant over different age groups. But beyond this general conclusion we still know little about the relationship between interest and understanding, between personality and understanding or response, and between the environment of the student and response.

E. Studies of the Process of Response

A very few studies have attempted to explore the process of an individual's response, what happens to the reader from when he picks up the work to when he finishes it. Many studies which touch upon this subject are introspective (e.g., Lesser, 1957; Holland, 1968; Purves, 1968; Slatoff, 1970) and may be valid descriptions of what happens to one individual. Holland's (1969) is perhaps the most comprehensive, for he explores his responses to several works over a period of time. A fairly strict Freudian, he poses a dualistic description, one which speaks of a logical—or at least conscious—process of analysis and interpretation, and one which speaks of a subconscious analogical reading of the fantasy of and in the work. These two processes interact in many complex ways to produce synthetic statements and evaluations of the work. His description supports that of other Freudians and psychological critics like Shrodes (1949), who posits a four-stage description: identification of the individual with the work (an affiliation with it), followed by a projection of the self into it, the emotional purging or catharsis, and the resultant intellectual or conscious insight. These four stages, Shrodes found, described the written responses of and the interviews with a number of young adult readers.

In a study of literary critics, Veley (1971) delineated some refinements of the stages: from passivity to involvement, from a primary emotion to an insight to a secondary emotion. This neat description, unfortunately, is more the *product* of response—the critical essay—than the *process*. If anything, Veley's pattern is a pattern of rhetorical discourse.

And there are many substages that need to be explored, substages about which Holland and Shrodes have hinted, such as the way in which identification is initiated, and the relationship between catharsis and insight (Loban, 1953). In addition, a follow-up of Downey's studies of self-projection needs to be made and probed. All of these require detailed case-study techniques.

Some studies begin to look at process in more specific ways, for example, the techniques of Squire, Hansson, and Dollerup, all of whom had students interrupt their readings either to speak or write their response or, in the case of Hansson, to check off responses to a series of scales. Hansson (1964) found that although the product of the response—the final statements—might vary among groups, the process of moving from one mental state to another during the course of reading was common to diverse groups of readers (university teachers, university students, people with a high school education). Dollerup's (1971) study of 26 university students, although only briefly reported in English, does indicate the cumulative nature of the reading process. It is quite obvious that much more research of the sort that Squire, Hansson, and Dollerup initiated needs to be undertaken.

A number of researchers have explored various facets of the larger question of the response process, including the response to aspects of literary works and other physical determinants of response. To take the latter group first, we find that little has been done recently. Peddie (1952) studied the responses of secondary school students with marked haptic tendencies (people with strong tactile or kinesthetic imaginations) and found they were better able to perform than other students on a test in which they had to complete poems according to fitness of mood. In an earlier study, Strother (1949) found a relation between muscle activity and types of poems read aloud: poems of fear provoked a higher reaction than poems of happiness, hate, and tranquillity. Nikiforova (1960) made one of the few studies of inner speech and literature, finding that if the reader of literary descriptions was accompanied by automotized speech activity, there was a decline in the quality of the students' judgments and drawings. Apparently constant articulation inhibits certain kinesthetic impulses. One of the most recent studies in this area (Kaiser, 1967) investigated the relation between metaphor and galvanic skin responses. Kaiser gave groups of elementary and secondary students one of two versions of a story—one with metaphor and one without. There were no differences between responses to the two stories.

Related to studies of physical response are those dealing with sounds and response. Although I. A. Richards argued that there was little emotion or meaning intrinsic in sounds, a number of empirical studies hint that some meaning or emotional value exists. One of the more extensive studies antedating Richards' work (Givler, 1915) found that different sounds produced different variations in rate (unpleasant sounds produced a faster rate) when subjects were asked to tap their fingers while reciting nonsense syllables and that there was fairly high reliability. Nonsense stanzas approximating poems were also recited and subjects gave consistent introspective impressions which correlated with the impressions gained after hearing the actual poem. His study confirmed an earlier one (Robler and Washburn, 1912) and was later replicated by Hevner (1937), who also found that metric changes produced distinctions in meaning, particularly in moving from iambic to anapestic rhythm. The most recent of these studies is 35 years old, however, and it seems odd that little has been done to follow up the studies and reexamine Richards' contention—accepted by many critics and teachers—that sound is not independent of meaning.

Studies dealing with the emotionality of words are somewhat more recent. In addition to general studies of reactions to words (e.g., Postman, Brewer, and McGinnis, 1948) which indicate that individual words do trigger specific reactions, a few researchers have looked at words in a literary context. Downey (1927) performed several studies, first classifying reactions to single nouns and adjectives as objective, associative, intra-subjective, symbolization, and personalization (giving character to a word—a series of classes not unlike many dealing with response to literature—and later (1929) a more important study showed that words tended to produce images in some people and emotional values in others. Broom (1966) made studies of emotional words in literary passages, asking students to select the word that best filled an emotional context and finding that the ability to do so was more highly correlated with reading than with other tests of emotion. In trying psycho-galvanic reactions to words in poems, Broom found there were reactions, "startles," given certain words but could not assert whether the word or the content was operating. One other study dealing with words and context showed that some words operate independently of context (Hinze, 1961). The words that interfere with the interpretation of passages are those about which the reader has mixed feelings. When the subject has a clear attitude toward a word, he tends to misinterpret a passage that uses that word with a contrary value. This power of words to affect response and understanding is slightly confounded by a study by Bormuth and MacDonald (1965) in which a "cloze" test was correlated with a test of the ability to detect style. This purely cognitive test was used with college students, and the two tests correlated. The ability to find the right word and to be objective about style, where people are called upon to demonstrate that ability, seems to transcend any personal associations with the words; one *can* refuse to be influenced by words, but most people do not seem to make that refusal.

There arises an equally confused picture from the studies related to imagery. The early studies of Peers (1913) and Downey (1929) asserted that people varied in the strength of their capacity to summon images and in the degree to which they were visual, audile, motile, or olfactive. Despite this difference, students who were presented images in poems primarily sensed visual images. The students' sense of images in a poem also increased when they understood the text, and students with a strong sense of images used it in understanding (or misunderstanding) a poem.

Provocative as these studies are, few researchers have sought to replicate or probe them, although Valentine, in another early study (1923), did conclude that students found imagery helped them to appreciate a text but that telling them to observe imagery hindered their sense of the whole poem and did not increase their enjoyment. One should also note that virtually nothing has been done to bring these separate studies together. Moran (1935) found weak correlations among tests of rhythm, imagery, and paraphrase (.16 to .48). But are the various aspects of understanding and response (sense of rhythm, sense of imagery, word association, understanding, reaction-type, and the like) all discrete? Do they form combinations in ways we don't quite know?

F. Studies in General Effects of Literature

There have been almost as many studies on what happens as a

result of reading literature as there have been on other aspects of response. Most have sought to test the hypothesis that writers exert an undue influence on readers and should, perhaps, be banned. Since we have arbitrarily limited ourselves to the printed book, we have excluded many related studies on comics, film, and television, which are the current battlefields for studies on influence. The studies on effect fall into two groups, those dealing with the general effects of books and literature and those dealing with the effects of specific texts.

Those works that deal with general effects have primarily explored the characteristics of the reader, the effects that he claims he experiences, and the satisfactions he senses. The following cataloging of satisfactions incorporates those cited by researchers (Lind, 1936; Waples, Berelson, and Bradshaw, 1940; Ford, 1961; and Shirley, 1966):

I. Instrumental (Lind; Waples, Berelson, and Bradshaw).
   A. Self-esteem or prestige, self-image (Shirley).

II. Emotional Pleasure.
   A. Diversion (Lind); emotional satisfaction (Ford).
   B. Escape (Lind, Ford); respite (Waples, Berelson, and Bradshaw).
   C. Sensitivity (Shirley).

III. Intellectual Pleasure.
   A. Aesthetic (Waples, Berelson, and Bradshaw); embodiment of beauty (Ford); self-defining (Lind).
   B. Intellectual stimulation (Ford); Knowledge of cultural groups, of politics, and of social problems (Shirley).
   C. Moral insight (Ford); reinforcement or conversion (Waples, Berelson, and Bradshaw); philosophy of life (Shirley).

In the Eight-Year Study, the matter of cataloging was approached differently and taxonomically (Smith, Tyler, et al., 1942):

1. Satisfaction in the thing appreciated.
2. Desire for more of the thing appreciated.
3. Desire to know more about the thing appreciated.
4. Desire to express one's self creatively.
5. Identification of one's self with the thing appreciated.
6. Desire to clarify one's thinking with regard to the life problems raised by the thing appreciated.
7. Desire to evaluate the thing appreciated.

In creating a measure of these desires, the committee drafted a 100-item questionnaire but reduced the categories to six, combining numbers 2 and 3. The instrument was tried with a small group and found reliable, but it was not used to any great extent. The classification is compatible with the preceding list but deals more with levels of satisfaction than with types of satisfaction. The two together form a valuable grid for further research, so that type and level could be studied together.

All of these researchers agree on the influence of social conditions on these effects, although Shirley significantly finds no correlation between type of influence and intelligence or reading ability. One influence that appears but which is not noted is that of the questionnaire situation. Ford's students are NCTE Achievement Award winners (so are those in a 1964 study by Whitman which produced similar results); the stated effects are more highly cognitive and aesthetic than are those cited in the other studies. This difference may result from the students themselves or from their perception of the questionnaire maker. In a recent British study, adolescents claimed that they read most for insight into other peoples' problems but were not interested in discussing literature (Yarlott and Harpin, 1971).

Two corollaries should be noted. In a study undertaken in 1948 to replicate an 1898 study of students' ideals, none of the 1,536 children reported ideals drawn from serious literature (3 percent from comics), a drop from the 1898 figure of 12 percent (Averill). Figures from sports, media, and trades replaced literary and historical figures. The study confirms that of Havighurst and Robinson. The second corollary study is that which deals with the focus of attitude changes (Smith, 1933). Her respondents, students in grades four through eight, reported that their attitudes changed toward people (37 percent) and animals (33 percent). Thirty percent told of revised thinking, and 9.2 percent actually mentioned a change in behavior. Smith's gathering of testimony indicates that people claim to change as a result of reading, but whether or not they do change is open to question.

The studies that take up this question in some detail come to no clear conclusion. A number indicate that after reading works dealing with selected topics people's attitudes toward those topics change (Sister Mary Agnes, 1946; Feltman, 1954; Young, 1963; Fisher, 1965; Tavran, 1967, inter al.), but a larger number indicate that their change is nonsignificant and short-lived (Lodge, 1953; Bovyer, 1962; Tatara, 1964; Brown, 1966; Milgrim, 1967; Holdsworth, 1968, inter al.). The latter group of studies, being better designed, seem to hold the most weight, so the case should be considered not proved, at least not generally proved, and such factors as length of time of exposure, recurrent exposure, and situation should be investigated.

Lewis (1967) went a bit deeper in that she checked the effect of various presentations. She presented sixth grade students with stories dealing with aggression, selfishness, and nurture: one group read and discussed them, a second group merely read them, a third group discussed the values, and a fourth group was the control group. Despite some inconsistencies, a general finding was that reading increased awareness of aggressive feelings (as measured by a semiprojective test) but that discussion after reading decreased these heightened feelings. Discussion alone brought no change. One implication is that discussion serves as a cathartic after reading so that the introduction of volatile material into a classroom should be followed by discussion to decrease tension.

One study (John and Barney, 1967) examined the psychological effect of telling ethnic stories to children of ethnic minorities. The effect on their self-image was sufficient to warrant inclusion of the materials in readers for non-Caucasian children.

G. Studies in Bibliotherapy

Bibliotherapy, the "process of dynamic interaction between the personality of the reader and literature as a psychological field which may be utilized for personality assessment, adjustment, and growth" (Shrodes, 1949), is a larger subarea of research, most of it case-study research rather than empirical or survey research. Shrodes did one of the pioneering studies in the area, and her work is a landmark, particularly for the survey information, the theoretical justification, and the elaborate case study it contains. Her study showed that the use of psychoanalytic techniques to probe the responses of individuals to literature could be as deep and penetrating as a probe through normal psychoanalytic techniques. Further, she showed that diagnosis of a student combined with prescribed reading and free response could effectively restructure the personality of the student.

Her study is supported by many other case studies (Wilson, 1951; Edgar, Hazley, and Levitt, 1969; Osthoff, 1970, to name but a few that follow the list compiled by Russell and Shrodes, 1950, and supplemented by Zaccaria and Moses, 1968, and Riggs, 1968). All of these studies indicate that a skillful teacher-therapist, using books—both literary and frankly didactic—prose, poetry, and drama, can effect a personality change in a neurotic patient. They can do so through the patient's identification with the character or situation, his/her projection of self into the vicarious situation, the resultant catharsis or emotional-psychological purging, and the resultant intellectual insight (see section E of this chapter for a comparison of this process description with others). The biblio-therapeutic stages seem to follow the general psychoanalytic stages or the stages of a patient-doctor relationship.

Whether bibliotherapy has any efficacy outside of the clinic has been the subject of a number of studies, generally empirical in nature. Some studies have shown the usefulness of the techniques in group therapy (Edgar and Hazley, 1969; Sapar, 1970), but what of the classroom? One study of eighth grade children found that there were significant changes in attitude as determined by various personality measures, particularly those dealing with social adjust-ment and aggressive behavior (Herminghaus, 1954). The research-ers did caution that there needed to be extensive teacher training. Amato (1957) made a study with college students who found bibliotherapy helpful, but his own research techniques, he finds, cast doubt on his findings. Osthoff (1969) found the technique use-ful in counselor training. Two studies found that sixth graders used books to help solve problems in daily living and that bibliothera-peutic techniques worked well in affecting behavior, particularly in changing "undemocratic" behavior (Livengood, 1961; Mattera, 1961). One recent study poses an interesting new direction for re-search in bibliotherapy. It was a study of the effectiveness of the technique with disadvantaged students, particularly with their degree of self-acceptance (Ponder, 1968). The results were what one might suspect—nonsignificant differences. The study was rigor-ously carried out, looking at the relationship of gain to teachers' scores on the same measures, to reading achievement, and the like. The treatment time was brief—one term—and may have been too little time in which to expect changes in this area. There might also have been too many negative influences counteracting the treat-ment. One suspects that the use of literature as a therapeutic agent may well be effective, but experimental research design will prob-ably not show its effectiveness. The case-study technique seems to be more acceptable proof, partly because the change will result from a set of variables so complex that the isolation of one will not show its effect and its interaction with others. Multiple regression and multiple discriminant analysis might help, but the case study seems the most efficacious sort of proof.

Bibliotherapy seems to be less a treatment or a classroom variable, in the traditional experimental sense, than it is a way of looking at literature and at the student. It is for this reason that studies are included in this section. Bibliotherapy considers the student as "unhealthy," in need of psychotherapy, and the book as a medium. The teacher becomes a therapist, on a par with a doctor. We question broadcasting of this idea throughout English classes, because we feel that it is both unwarranted and infeasible. What we do not question, however, is the attitude of the bibliotherapist, an attitude that Shrodes imparts so well. This attitude implies that careful analytic techniques—in this case Freudian techniques—must be applied not only to the literature but also to the oral and written responses of students. The amount of information about her subject that Shrodes imparts through her technique is amazing. If a teacher considers what his students say and write with half as much thoroughness, then knowledge gained and the impact upon teaching and learning may well be strong. Such a technique tends to help the teacher approach each student as an individual.

H. Studies of the Factors in Literary Learning

This section deals with a series of miscellaneous studies which are neither fully descriptive nor analytic nor treatment studies. Smith (1941), for example, sought to ascertain what contributed to increased appreciation of literature, as determined by questionnaires and interviews with mature "appreciators." He reported that mental attitude and clarity of objectives for the learner were more important than the qualities of the work to be read. Ninety-four percent of the people believed that comprehension of meaning was all of appreciation, followed by ability to create word pictures and associate emotions. Least important was the knowledge of literary-critical terms. A more direct study (Wheeler, 1923) asked university students to note any images that struck them as they read two poems three times. They were then asked whether noting the images "naturally" was useful. Eighty percent said that the continuity of images was useful to this appreciation. When asked to make an effort to obtain images as they read, 74 percent reported the effort hindered their appreciation. This indication of the interference of enforced analysis with a sense of the wholeness of the poem, put together with Valentine's early report (1923), gives us some information about attitudes toward the study of literature, but we need to know more to find out whether the often expressed distaste for such study is as widespread a phenomenon as the loudest complainers in any class would have us believe. Kammann (1966) found that perceived task influenced choice; students would choose to explore texts that were relatively simple if they had to face a teacher; if the choice were for discussion with a friend, the choice would be for a more complex text. Further, the students' interest declined when they considered they had to read the poem for a professor and rose as anxiety about the assignment was reduced. His study certainly deserves amplification.

There have been a few studies of knowledge of authors and work. In 1947 White found that knowledge correlated .69 with reading ability when twelfth grade urban students were tested. A small study of knowledge of fairy tales (Babcock, 1949) found that young children knew a good number of the classics and liked them. A more fruitful study (Witzig, 1956) tested whether students remembered mythical prose longer than factual prose. He applied a measure using four selections and a week's time lag and found that the factual material faded somewhat faster than the mythological, a very modest confirmation of the Jungian hypothesis about the power of the collective unconscious.

An early study (Burch, 1928) sought to define levels along three dimensions: understanding ideas, sharing the experience of the characters, and entering the vicarious experience. A test, controlled for reading difficulty, distinguished grades eight, nine, and ten from grades eleven and twelve. This study is one of the few developmental studies undertaken, and it badly needs to be redone, adding more modern material and considering other dimensions.

One related study (Bailey, 1955) deserves separate attention, partly because it deals with the specialized topic of Bible study. Bailey examined the relationship between social and personal characteristics of adolescents and their comprehension of Bible passages. Students were asked to read and write answers to questions about meaning and personal applications of biblical passages and to relate the passages to modern life. The ability to read and relate was correlated with intelligence, formal Bible study, and church attendance (but not with sex and age). Which of the three positive correlates accounted for more of the variance was not determined, but study seems to confirm the notion that prior exposure, either formal or informal, improves understanding (as measured by an expert judgment of what understanding should be).

Obviously, a great deal of research could be done that would probe relationships among the various aspects of literary achievement. The National Assessment data may prove of some help in this matter when it comes out, but because of the nature of the sampling, multiple analysis of variance or multiple correlation will probably not be forthcoming. Certainly a series of carefully related studies would be useful.

I. Development of Literature Tests

There are some few studies in which the prime emphasis has been on the development of test measures themselves (see the recent review by Cooper, 1971). Each of these assumes the isolatability of certain behaviors related to literary achievement. More often than not the behaviors are isolated by happenstance or by custom. Thus one testmaker (Lawson, 1968) assumes that the ability to comprehend the meaning, the ability to identify the technicalities of verse, and the ability to make value judgments are the three "appropriate" behaviors for testing achievement with respect to poetry. The resultant test is reliable, difficult, and relatively valid (r. 71 with semester grades of eleventh and twelfth grade students). Lawson's global descriptions of abilities hide a multiplicity of subbehaviors, however, and one wonders how adequate a sampling of these behaviors there was. The same criticism may be applied to other formulations of test items; *A Look at Literature* (NCTE/Educational Testing Service, 1969), classifies items in an "appreciation" test under translation, extension, and awareness. When nine experts were asked to classify the items, they could secure 55 percent agreement on 91 percent of the items but 86 percent agreement on only 37 percent of the items. Finer classification schemes are needed, but the NCTE/ETS test does seem to provide an adequate measure of the ability of fourth and fifth grade students to read literary passages with some understanding. No validity measures were undertaken, but KR-20 reliability estimates were found to be .83. The correlation of the test with the STEP reading test ranges from .67 to .79, indicating that the test is not greatly different from a general measure of reading ability. This finding contradicts those of Forman (1951) who found the correlation to be .53, and Hartley (1930) who found it to be lower. Hartley's study made finer classifications in a test of meaning by taking passages that show problems with syntactic condensation, e.g., problems with figures and symbols, sense impressions, word values, and rhythm, and making up one four-choice item pertinent to that problem for each passage.

These studies dealt with multiple-choice tests, a form convenient to the statistician but anathema to the humanist. Two studies have sought to validate multiple-choice against "freer" test measures. One found that multiple-choice items on a poem and a short story correlated no higher than .23 with scores on short answers and essay questions (Sterling, 1967). This finding was confirmed by Choppin and Purves (1969), but they found that when the items were matched—multiple-choice against short-answer—and when stories were the stimuli, the correlations rose from .39 to .60. These correlations attenuated for unreliability range from .58 to .91. "The multiple-choice questions per se do not seem to measure anything different than open-ended questions per se." What differences exist seem to be between the stimulus texts rather than between item-types, so that one cannot easily castigate multiple-choice items.

Another kind of test that was developed for its own sake is the test of the ability to empathize with literary characters (Mahoney, 1960). Such a test was a series of 20 multiple-choice items on each of four passages; the subjects were to answer the items as they thought the character might. The scores were slightly correlated with other empathy measures, and more highly correlated with tests of reading. These results indicated that the test might have been measuring the ability to comprehend a character rather than the ability to empathize. Still another kind is that of Howells and Johnson (1932), who tested the ability to discriminate among types of metre and created a measure that differentiated high school and college students.

We have referred to measures of taste and other aspects of literary response in the sections specifically directed to those topics. We should note the various attempts to create measures of taste, specifically those of Abbott and Trabue, Rigg, Herbert Carroll, and Ash. All worked on measures with "best" or "more literary" selections and some distortions. Of these Carroll's is the least satisfactory because it does not consider the interrelation of form and content but uses four different selections, each one representative of a different "level" of style in Carroll's terms (a different order of style to the reader). Abbott and Trabue, Rigg, and Ash used much more valid techniques, and their measures (or versions of them) should be used in research, although perhaps with less judgmental sorts of interpreting.

We should note other measures developed as instruments for other studies, particularly those developed for curriculum evaluation. The instruments created for the Eight-Year Study in attitudes and interest (Smith and Tyler, 1942) and those developed by Fader and McNeil (1968) for "English in Every Classroom," a curriculum project sponsored by Program English of the United States Office of Education, are as good as any in the field. The measures created for the Carnegie Curriculum Project (Steinberg et al., 1968) are examples of measures of cognitive style. Certainly these, as well as the cognitive measures developed by Coryell, Hartley, and the Florida State Curriculum Project (Burton et al., 1968), and those referred to in this section should all be considered for any evaluative task or any research study. (See chapter 3 for a fuller discussion of this topic.) Other sources on the development of testing instruments and test design in literature may be found in Bloom, Hastings, and Madaus (1971).

Summary

What, then, do we know about response to literature? We know that it is a complex process and that it consists of a number of interrelated parts: understanding; the possession of information and the ability to grasp verbal and human complexities; psychological readiness to become as objective as one can; the concomitant psychological ability to enter into the world of the work; the use of various evaluative criteria, both personal and impersonal; and the ability to articulate critical statements. We know that understanding and liking are associated. We know that readers are interested more in the content of literature than in its form. We know that some readers can be influenced by what they read—emotionally, attitudinally, and intellectually.

The studies also tend to support the transactional theory of criticism set forth by Rosenblatt, who drew on Dewey and Bentley's transactional formulation for the natural sciences. This theory states that there are a text and an individual reader and that the transaction between the two produces the poem. That the resultant poem is dominated almost equally by the two forces seems demonstrated by a number of studies, but it is also the operating assumption of a number, those which examine reader variables holding the text constant or text variables holding the reader constant. That this assumption lies at the heart of most of the studies is no criticism of the studies but simply an acknowledgment of one of the "tacit assumptions"—to use Polanyi's phrase—in this research. Only a few of the taste studies seem to question the assumption, because they do take for granted the unassailable quality of the text. A skeptic can say, however, that what is unassailable is not the text but the judgment of the researchers. Similarly, some of the tests of comprehension assume a "right answer" to their questions, but one can say that answers are not right or wrong, but more or less reasonable. With these two possible exceptions, however, the researchers in response to literature have generally accepted and confirmed the transactionist definition.

If we construct a chart of the four schemata we have set forth in this chapter, one finds a number of significant correspondences. The schemata of understanding, judgment, response, and satisfaction all contain cognitive and personal aspects, or perhaps "objective" and "subjective." All seem to recognize a split between form and content as they are understood, judged, perceived, and appreciated. There is an evaluation aspect to all of the schemata, which seems to be both understanding and judgment and which seems to be both personal and impersonal. If we place the categories from these schemata together with the four stages of the process of response, we see even more exciting connections.

Understanding	Judgment	Response	Process of Response	Satisfaction
Information lack	General liking	Personal	Identification	Instrumental
Cognitive failure	Formal liking	Descriptive	Projection	Pleasure (Intellectual)
Psychological block	Liking of content	Interpretive	Catharsis	Pleasure (Emotional)
	Personal judgment	Evaluative	Insight	

Certainly at both a theoretical and an empirical level, much more needs to be done to probe the connections among these five general areas. What is the relation between catharsis and emotional pleasure, or personal response and the psychological blocks to understanding? What is the relationship of formal liking to cognitive failure or mastery? What are the relationships between the variously derived but similar subcategories of the five areas? Many more studies of interrelationships are needed if we are to move any closer to an understanding of the complexity of response to literature.

The next direction in research, thus, might well be exploration into the complex system of literary response. Such exploration might well employ the case-study technique of exploring many aspects of the responses of a few individuals. This technique should be combined with multivariate analysis, multidimensional scaling, partition analysis, and other more sophisticated statistical treatments. The simple correlation tells us some things, but not enough. Further, some early studies should be not simply replicated but deepened. The studies of Vine, Britton, Ash, Meckel, Downey, Thayer and Pronko, Stewart, Hansson, Loban, Shrodes, Givler, Kammann, Shirley—to name but a few—are among those which should be reexamined, rethought, and repeated. All of them raise interesting questions, all suggest ways of answering questions, all need the application of new methodological techniques to find answers.

Each of the questions and answers has an impact on the teaching of literature. In part, they can help the teacher know about text selection. More important, however, they can tell the teacher about how and why students approach literature as they do and about what kinds of questions to ask of students. Many of the studies deal with the verbalization of response and its relation to perception. Knowing the types of verbalization and of perception that are most to be expected, as well as the possible disturbances and sources of confusion, can only help a teacher interested in the cognitive and affective growth of students.

Bibliography

A *Look at Literature*. The Research Foundation of the National Council of Teachers of English, Urbana, Illinois, and the Educational Testing Service, Princeton, New Jersey, 1969.

Abbott, Allan, and M. R. Trabue. "A Measure of Ability to Judge Poetry." *Teachers College Record* 22 (March 1921), 101-126.

Abrams, Meyer. *The Mirror and the Lamp*. New York: Oxford University Press, 1953.

Allen, Edward. "Books Help Neuropsychiatric Patients." *Library Journal* 71 (1946), 1671-1675.

Alpert, Harvey. "The Relationship of Empathy to Reading Comprehension in Selected Content Fields." Diss. University of Florida, 1955.

Amato, Anthony J. "Some Effects of Bibliotherapy on Young Adults." Diss. Pennsylvania State University, 1957.

Ash, Brian. "The Construction of an Instrument to Measure Some Aspects of Literary Judgment and Its Use as a Tool to Investigate Student Responses to Literature." Diss. Syracuse University, 1969.

Averill, Lawrence A. "The Impact of a Changing Culture upon Pubescent Ideals." *School and Society* 72 (July 1950), 49-53.

Babcock, Mildred D. "What Children Know about Fairy Tales." *Elementary English* 26 (May 1949), 265-267.

Bailey, Frances E. "The Responses of Adolescents to Selected Bible

Passages: The Ability of Youth to Relate the Bible to Its Concerns." Diss. University of California at Berkeley, 1955.

Barrett, C. Patricia and G. V. "Enjoyment of Stories in Terms of Role Identification." *Perceptual and Motor Skills* 23 (1966), 1164.

Bauer, Edith B. "The Interrelatedness of Personality and Achievement in Reading." Diss. University of California at Berkeley, 1956.

Berelson, Bernard. "The Public Library, Book Reading, and Political Behavior." *Library Quarterly* 15 (1945), 281-299.

Berninghausen, D. K., and R. W. Faunce. "Exploring Study of Juvenile Delinquency and the Reading of Sensational Books." *Journal of Experimental Education* 33 (Winter 1964), 161-168.

Berstein, Margery R. "Relationship between Interest and Reading Comprehension." *Journal of Educational Research* 49 (December 1955), 283-289.

Betsky, S. "Literature and General Culture." *University Quarterly* 15 (December 1960), 34-45.

Beverley, Clara. "Poetry Appreciation." *Detroit Journal of Education* (October 1922), 67-72.

Black, E. L. "The Difficulty of Training College Students in Understanding What They Read." *British Journal of Educational Psychology* 24 (1954), 17-31.

Blair, Elizabeth H. "Establishment of a Basis for Testing in Literature with Partial Standardization of the Tests Constructed." *University of Pittsburgh Bulletin* 29 (January 1933), 45-52.

Bloom, Benjamin, J. Thomas Hastings, and George Madaus. *Handbook of Formative and Summative Evaluation of Student Learning*. New York: McGraw-Hill, 1971.

Bormuth, J. R., and O. L. MacDonald. "Cloze Tests as a Measure of Ability to Detect Literary Style." In *Reading and Inquiry,* Proceedings of the IRA. Edited by J. A. Figurel, pp. 287-290. Newark, Delaware: International Reading Association, 1965.

Bovyer, George G. "Stories and Children's Concepts of Sportsmanship in the Fourth, Fifth, and Sixth Grades." *Elementary English* 39 (December 1962), 762-765.

Boyd, Nancy A., and George Mandler. "Children's Responses to Human and Animal Stories and Pictures." *Journal of Consulting Psychology* 19 (1955), 367-371.

Brisbin, Charles D. *"An Experimental Application of the Galvanic Skin Response to the Measurement of Effects of Literature on Attitudes of Fifth Grade Students toward Blacks."* Diss. Wayne State University, 1971.

Britton, J. N. "Evidence of Improvement in Poetic Judgment." *The British Journal of Psychology* 45 (1954), 196-208.

Broom, M. E. "A Study of Literary Appreciation." *Journal of Applied Psychology* 18 (1934), 357-363.

Brown, Pauline. "The Relationship of Attitude and Reading Comprehension to Critical Reading Response." Diss. Boston University, 1966.

Bruner, Jerome, and L. Postman. "Emotional Selectivity in Perception and Reaction." *Journal of Personality* 16 (1947), 69-77.

Buehler, John A., Jr. "Change in Appropriateness of Affective Responses as a Function of Prior Affective Responses." Thesis. University of California, 1952.

Burch, Mary C. "Determination of a Content of the Course in Literature of a Suitable Difficulty for Junior and Senior High School Students." *Genetic Psychology,* Monographe 4, nos. 2 & 3 (1928).

Burgdorff, Arlene B. "A Study of the Ability of Intermediate-Grade

Children to Draw Inferences from Selections of Children's Literature." Diss. Ball State University, 1966.

Carroll, Herbert A. "Appreciation of Literature and Abstract Intelligence." *Journal of Educational Psychology* 25 (January 1934), 54-57.

_____. "Influence of the Sex Factor upon Appreciation of Literature." *School and Society* 27 (April 1933), 468-472.

_____. "A Method of Measuring Prose Appreciation." *English Journal* 22 (1933), 184-189.

Carroll, John B. "A Factor Analysis of Literary Style." *Personality Factors in the Development of Communication and Leadership Skills.* Final Report, Project No. 217. Harvard University, May 1968.

_____. *From Comprehension to Inference.* Princeton, New Jersey: Educational Testing Service, May 1969. Research Memorandum RM 69-11.

_____. "Vectors of Prose Style." In *Style in Language.* Edited by Thomas A. Sebeok, pp. 282-292. New York: Wiley, 1960.

Chandler, Henry B., and John T. Croteau. *A Regional Library and Its Readers: A Study of Five Years of Reading.* New York: American Association for Adult Education, 1940.

Choppin, Bruce. "Can Literary Appreciation Be Measured Objectively?" *International Review of Education* 15 (1969), 241-247.

Choppin, Bruce, and Alan C. Purves. "A Comparison of Open-ended and Multiple-choice Items Dealing with Literary Understanding." *Research in the Teaching of English* 3 (1969), 15-24.

Cooper, Charles R. "Preferred Modes of Literary Response: The Characteristics of High School Juniors in Relation to the Consistency of Their Reactions to Three Dissimilar Short Stories." Diss. University of California at Berkeley, 1969.

————. "Measuring Appreciation of Literature: A Review of Attempts." *Research in the Teaching of English* 5 (1971), 5-23.

Crossen, Helen J. "Effect of Attitudes of the Reader upon Critical Reading Ability." Diss. University of Chicago, 1946.

————. "Effects of the Attitudes of the Reader upon Critical Reading Ability." *Journal of Educational Research* 42 (December 1948), 289-298.

Curtis, William J. "An Analysis of the Relationship of Illustration and Text in Picture-Story Books as Indicated by the Oral Responses of Young Children." Diss. Wayne State University, 1968.

Davis, Frederick B. "Fundamental Factors of Comprehension in Reading." *Psychometrika* 9 (September 1944), 186.

Dieckmann, Hans. "Childhood's Favorite Fairy Tale and Its Relation to Neurosis and Personality Structure." *Praxis der Kinderpsychologie und Kinderpsychiatrie* 16 (1967), 202-208.

Dill, Nancy A., and Alan C. Purves, with J. Weiss and A. W. Foshay. *The Teaching of Literature.* Report of the U.S. National Committee for the International Educational Achievement Literature Project. Chicago, Illinois: University of Chicago, 1967. Available through ERIC(ED 039 399; EDRS price: microfiche-$0.65, hard copy-$3.29, 62p. Write ERIC Document Reproduction Service, P.O. Box 0, Bethesda, Maryland 20014).

Dollerup, Cay. "On Reading Short Stories." *Journal of Reading* 14 (1971), 445-454.

Downey, June. *Creative Imagination: Studies in the Psychology of Literature.* London: Kegan, Paul, Trench, Trubner and Company, 1929.

————. "Individual Differences in Reaction to the Word-in-Itself." *American Journal of Psychology* 39 (1927), 323-342.

Early, Margaret J. "Literature and the Development of Reading

Skills." Paper presented at the International Reading Association Conference. Boston, Massachusetts, 1968.

Edgar, Kenneth F., and Richard Hazley. "Validation of Poetry Therapy as a Group Therapy Technique." In *Poetry Therapy: The Use of Poetry in the Treatment of Emotional Disorders.* Edited by Jack J. Leedy, pp. 111-123. Philadelphia, Pennsylvania: J. P. Lippincott, 1969.

Edgar, Kenneth F., Richard Hazley, and Herbert I. Levitt. "Poetry Therapy with Hospitalized Schizophrenics." In *Poetry Therapy: The Use of Poetry in the Treatment of Emotional Disorders.* Edited by Jack J. Leedy, pp. 29-37. Philadelphia, Pennsylvania: J. P. Lippincott, 1969.

Eisenman, Sister Mary Victoria. "An Exploratory Study to Investigate the Values of Literature as Experienced by Elementary Parochial School Children and Teachers in the Diocese of Covington." Diss. St. Louis University, 1962.

Elkind, Samuel. "High School Drama as Self-Discovery." Diss. Teachers College, Columbia University, 1963.

Ellis, Katherine. "A New Approach to the Interpretation of Stories as Projective Documents." Diss. Columbia University, 1951.

Eppel, E. M. "A New Test of Poetry Discrimination." *British Journal of Educational Psychology* 20 (1950), 111-116.

Evans, Eleanor M. "Objective Tests in Eighth Grade Literature." *Elementary English* 5 (January 1928), 13-22.

Evans, John Lyle. "Two Aspects of Literary Appreciation among High School Students, Judgment of Prose Quality and Emotional Responses to Literature, and Selected Aspects of Their Reading Interests." Diss. University of Minnesota, 1968.

Eysenck, H. J. "Some Factors in the Appreciation of Poetry, and Their Relation to Temperamental Qualities." *Character and Personality* 9 (1940-1941), 160-167.

Fanselow, John F. "The Responses of Ninth Grade Bilingual Adolescents to Four Short Stories." Diss. Columbia University, 1971.

Feasey, Lynette. "Children's Appreciation of Poems." *British Journal of Psychology* 18 (1927), 51-68.

Feltman, Irene. "Study of Fiction as Source Material in Vocational Guidance." Diss. University of Illinois, 1954.

Figurel, J. Allen. "Relative Difficulty of Reading Material for Ninth Grade Literature." *Pittsburgh Schools* 16 (January-February 1942), 125-138.

Fisher, Frank L. "The Influences of Reading and Discussion on Attitudes of Fifth Graders toward American Indians." Diss. University of California at Berkeley, 1965.

Flournoy, Henri. "Poetry and Childhood Memory." *International Journal of Psycho-Analysis* 30 (1949), 206.

Ford, N. A. "What High School Students Say about Good Books." *English Journal* 50 (November 1961), 539-540.

Forman, Earl. "An Instrument to Evaluate the Literary Appreciation of Adolescents." Diss. University of Illinois, 1951.

Foster, Jeannette H. "An Approach to Fiction through the Characteristics of Its Readers." *The Library Quarterly* 6 (April 1936), 124-174.

Fredholm, A. "Gymnasisters Litterära Värderingskriterier." *Svensklärarföreningens Arsskrift* (1970), 61-100.

Frye, Northrop. *Anatomy of Criticism.* Princeton, New Jersey: Princeton University Press, 1957.

Gans, Roma A. "A Study of Critical Reading Comprehension in the Intermediate Grades." *Teachers College Contributions to Education,* no. 811. New York: Bureau of Publications, Teachers College, Columbia University, 1940.

Garrison, K. C., and Mabel Thomas. "A Study of Some Literature

Appreciation Abilities as They Relate to Certain Vocabulary Abilities." *Journal of Educational Research* 22 (December 1930), 396-399.

Givler, Robert C. "The Psycho-Physiological Effect of the Elements of Speech in Relation to Poetry." *Psychology Review Monographs* 19 (1915), 1-132.

Glasgow, George. "The Relative Effects of Distinct and Indistinct Enunciation on Audiences' Comprehension of Prose and Poetry." *Journal of Educational Research* 37 (December 1943), 263-267.

Glicksberg, C. I. "Psychology and the Teaching of English." *Peabody Journal of Education* 21 (1944), 284-295.

Grace, Harry A., and Joan J. Lohmann. "Children's Reactions to Stories Depicting Parent-Child Conflict Situations." *Child Development* 23 (March 1952), 61-74.

Gray, William S. "The Social Effects of Reading." *School Review* 55 (1947), 269-277.

Groff, Patrick J. "Children's Attitudes toward Reading and Their Critical Reading Abilities in Four Content-Type Materials." Diss. University of California at Berkeley, 1955.

Gunn, Douglas G. "Factors in the Appreciation of Poetry." *British Journal of Educational Psychology* 21 (1951), 96-104.

Hallowell, A. J. "Cultural Factors in the Structuralization of Perception." In *Social Psychology at the Crossroads*. Edited by J. H. Rohrer and M. Sherif, pp. 164-195. New York: Harper, 1951.

_____. "Myth Culture and Personality." *American Anthropology* 44 (1947), 544-556.

Hansen, Harlan S. "The Relationship between the Home Literary Environment and Self-Commitment to Independent Reading." Diss. University of Wisconsin, 1967.

Hansson, Gunnar. *Dikten Och Läsaren: Studier Över Diktupplevelsen.* Stockholm, Sweden (1959), 1970.

———. *Dikt I Profil.* Göteborg, Sweden, 1964.

———. *Författaren—Dikton—Läsaren.* Stockholm, Sweden, 1969.

———. "Med Undervisning Och Utan." *Svensklärarföreningens Arsskrift* (1970), 45-60.

Harding, D. W. "Practice at Liking: A Study in Experimental Aesthetics." *Bulletin of the British Psychology Society* 21 (January 1960), 3-10.

Harpin, W. S. "The Appreciation of Prose: Measurement and Evaluation with Special Reference to the Novel, Using the Semantic Differential." *Educational Review* 19 (November 1966), 13-22.

Harris, Chester W. "Measurement of Comprehension of Literature I." *School Review* 56 (1948), 280-289.

———. "Measurement of Comprehension of Literature II." *School Review* 56 (1948), 332-342.

———. "Measurement of Comprehension of Literature and Its Relation to Enjoyment." Diss. University of Chicago, 1946.

Hartley, Helene. "Tests for Interpretative Reading of Poetry for Teachers of English." *Teachers College Contributions to Education*, no. 433. New York: Bureau of Publications, Teachers College, Columbia University, 1930.

Havighurst, Robert J., Mary Z. Robinson, and Mildred Dorr. "The Development of the Ideal Self in Childhood and Adolescence." *Journal of Educational Research* 40 (December 1946), 241-257.

Hayes, Marie T. "An Investigation of the Impact of Reading on Attitudes of Racial Prejudice." Diss. Boston University, 1969.

Heisler, Florence. "A Comparison between Those Elementary School Children Who Attend Movie Pictures, Read Comic Books, and Listen to Serial Radio Programs to Excess, with Those Who Indulge in These Activities Seldom or Not at All." *Journal of Educational Research* 42 (1948), 182-190.

Herminghaus, Earl G. "The Effect of Bibliotherapy on the Attitudes and Personal and Social Adjustment of a Group of Elementary School Children." Diss. Washington University, 1954.

Hevner, Kate. "An Experimental Study of the Affective Value of Sounds in Poetry." *American Journal of Psychology* 49 (1937), 419-434.

Hinze, Helen K. "The Individual's Word Associations and His Interpretation of Prose Paragraphs." *Journal of General Psychology* 64 (1961), 193-203.

Hogue, Bradley B., Jr. "Some Effects of a Reader Written for Children from Families of Low Socio-Economic Circumstances." Diss. North Texas State University, 1964.

Holdsworth, Janet N. "Vicarious Experience of Reading a Book in Changing Nursing Students' Attitudes." *Nursing Research* 17 (1968), 135-139.

Holland, Norman. *The Dynamics of Literary Response.* New York: Oxford University Press, 1969.

Holm, I. *Drama Pa Scen.* Stockholm, Sweden, 1969.

Horne, Rose N. "A Study of the Use of Figurative Language by Sixth Grade Children." Diss. University of Georgia, 1966.

Howells, Thomas H., and Allean A. Johnson. "A Study of Metre-Sense in Poetry." *The Journal of Applied Psychology* 15 (1932), 539-544.

Husband, J. D. "A Technique for the Evaluation of Growth in Certain Affective Phases of Reading among High School Pupils." *Journal of Educational Research* 39 (1945), 265-271.

Ingram, Charles O. "How University Freshmen Read: A Study of the Dynamics of the Reading Process." Diss. University of Arizona, 1967.

Irion, Theo. W. H. "Comprehension Difficulties of Ninth Grade Students in the Study of Literature." *Teachers College Contri-*

butions to Education, no. 189. New York: Bureau of Publications, Teachers College, Columbia University, 1925.

Jackson, Evalene P. "Effects of Reading upon Attitudes toward the Negro Race." *Library Quarterly* 14 (January 1944), 47-54.

Jahoda, Marie. *The Impact of Literature: A Psychological Discussion of Some Assumptions in the Censorship Debate.* New York: Research Center for Human Relations, 1954.

Jay, Edith S. "A Factor Study of Reading Tasks." Diss. University of Chicago, 1950.

Jenkinson, Marion D. "Selected Processes and Difficulties of Reading Comprehension." Diss. University of Chicago, 1957.

John, Vera P., and Tomi D. Berney. *Analysis of Story Retelling as a Measure of the Effects of Ethnic Content in Stories.* New York: Yeshiva University, 1967.

Kaiser, Robert A. "Student Physiological Response to Metaphor in Reading." Diss. University of Pittsburgh, 1967.

Kammann, Richard. "Verbal Complexity and Preferences in Poetry." *Journal of Verbal Learning and Verbal Behavior* 5 (1966), 536-540.

Keneally, Katherine. "Therapeutic Value of Books." In *Youth Communications and Libraries,* pp. 69-77. Chicago, Illinois: American Library Association, 1949.

Kingston, A. J., and W. F. White. "The Relationship of Readers' Self Concepts and Personality Components to Semantic Meanings Perceived in the Protagonist of a Reading Selection." *Reading Research Quarterly* 2 (1967), 107-116.

Lawson, James H. "The Development of a Poetry Test for Grades Eleven and Twelve." Diss. University of Kansas, 1968.

Lazarfeld, Sofie. "The Use of Fiction in Psychotherapy." *American Journal of Psychotherapy* 3 (1949), 26-33.

Leopold, Kathleen B. "The Effects of Creative Work on Aesthetic Appreciation." *British Journal of Educational Psychology* 3 (1933), 42.

Lesser, Simon O. *Fiction and the Unconscious.* New York: Random House, 1957.

Letton, Mildred C. "Individual Differences in Interpretive Responses in Reading Poetry at the Ninth Grade Level." Diss. University of Chicago, 1958.

Lewis, Isabel R. "Some Effects of the Reading and Discussion of Stories on Certain Values of Sixth Grade Pupils." Diss. University of California at Berkeley, 1967.

Lewis, Ralph. "Books That Germans Are Reading about America." *Library Quarterly* 29 (October 1959), 246-250.

Lind, K. N. "The Social Psychology of Children's Reading." *American Journal of Sociology* 41 (1936), 454-469.

Lindholm, S. *Att Uppleva Metaforer.* Stockholm, Sweden, 1963.

Livengood, Dorothy K. "The Effect of Bibliotherapy upon Peer Relations and Democratic Practices in a Sixth Grade Classroom." Diss. University of Florida, 1961.

Livingston, Howard. "Responding to Poetry." *Missouri English Bulletin* (October 1968), 11-13.

Loban, Walter. "Adolescents of Varying Sensitivity and Their Responses to Literature Intended to Evoke Sympathy." Diss. University of Minnesota, 1949.

———. "A Study of Social Sensitivity (Sympathy) among Adolescents." *Journal of Educational Psychology* 44 (February 1953), 102-112.

———. *Literature and Social Sensitivity.* Urbana, Illinois: National Council of Teachers of English, 1953.

Lodge, Helen. "The Influence of the Study of Biography on the

Moral Ideology of the Adolescent at the Eighth Grade Level."
Diss. University of California at Berkeley, 1953.

————. "The Influence of the Study of Biography on the Moral
Ideology of the Adolescent at the Eighth Grade Level." *Journal
of Educational Research* 50 (1956), 241-255.

Lorang, Sister Mary Carle. "The Effect of Reading on Moral Con-
duct and Emotional Experience." In *Studies in Psychology and
Psychiatry* 6, no. 5. Washington, D.C.: Catholic University Press,
1945.

McCaul, Robert L. "The Effect of Attitudes upon Reading Interpretation." *Journal of Educational Research* 37 (February 1944),
451-457.

McKillop, Anne S. "The Relationship between the Reader's Attitude and Certain Types of Reading Responses." Diss. Columbia
University, 1951.

Mahoney, Stanley C. "The Literature Empathy Test: Development
of a Procedure for Differentiating between 'Good Empathizers'
and 'Poor Empathizers.' " Diss. University of Oklahoma, 1960.

Marie Therese, Sister. "Bibliotherapy in the Elementary Classroom." *Catholic School Journal* 55 (February 1954), 35-37.

Mary Agnes, Sister. "Bibliotherapy for Socially Maladjusted Children." *Catholic Education Review* 44 (1946), 8-15.

————. "Influence of Reading on the Racial Attitudes of Adolescent Girls." *Catholic Education Review* 45 (September 1947),
415-420.

Matson, Elson L. "A Study of Years of Formal Education as a
Factor in Audience Response to Ideational Content and Treatment in Plays." Diss. State University of Iowa, 1953.

Mattera, Gloria. "Bibliotherapy in a Sixth Grade." Diss. Pennsylvania State University, 1961.

Meckel, H. C. "An Exploratory Study of the Responses of Adolescent Pupils to Situations in a Novel." Diss. University of Chicago, 1946.

Michael, William B., Bernard Rosenthal, and Michael DeCamp. "An Experimental Investigation of Prestige-Suggestion for Two Types of Literary Material." *Journal of Psychology* 28 (1949), 303-323.

Milgrim, Sally A. "A Comparison of the Effects of Classics and Contemporary Literary Works on High School Students' Declared Attitudes toward Certain Moral Values." Diss. New York University, 1967.

Monson, Dianne L. "Children's Responses to Humorous Situations in Literature." Diss. University of Minnesota, 1966.

Moran, Mary C. "Construction of Three Tests Designed to Measure Certain Poetry Aptitudes of Teachers of English at the High School Level Holding an A.B. or B.S. Degree or Better." *Teachers College Journal* 6 (March 1935), 139-167.

Morris, William P. "Unstructured Oral Responses of Experienced Readers Reacting to a Given Poem." Diss. Indiana University, 1970.

Nikiforova, O. I. "Role of Inner Speech in the Reconstruction of Literary Images." Translated Abstract, *Psychological Abstracts* 34 (1960), 395-396.

Osthoff, Irene. "The Use of Literature in Training Counsellors." Diss. University of Illinois, 1969.

Patrick, Catherine. "How Responses to Good and Poor Poetry Differ." *Journal of Psychology* 8 (October 1939), 253-283.

Peddie, Richard L. "The Relation of Haptic Perception to Literary Creative Work." *British Psychological Society Bulletin* 3 (1952), 19-21.

Peers, E. Allison. "Imagery in Imaginative Literature." *The Journal of Experimental Pedagogy* 2 (1913), 174-187, 261-280.

Philip, B. R. "The Effect of General and Specific Labelling on Judgmental Scales." *Canadian Journal of Psychology* 5 (1951), 18-28.

Pickford, R. W. "Some Mental Functions Illustrated by an Experiment on Reading—Part I." *British Journal of Psychology* 25 (April 1935), 417-435.

————. "Some Mental Functions Illustrated by an Experiment on Reading—Part II." *British Journal of Psychology* 26 (July 1935), 49-58.

Pierce-Jones, J. "Reading and Children's Adjustment." Diss. University of Oregon, 1954.

Pollock, John C. "A Study of Responses to Short Stories by Selected Groups of Ninth Graders, Eleventh Graders, and College Freshmen." Diss. University of Colorado, 1969.

Ponder, Virginia B. "An Investigation of the Effects of Bibliotherapy and Teachers' Self-Others Acceptance on Pupils' Self-Acceptance and Reading Achievement Scores." Diss. University of Southern Mississippi, 1968.

Postman, L., J. Bruner, and E. McGinnies. "Personal Values as Selective Factors in Perception." *Journal of Abnormal and Social Psychology* 43 (1948), 142-154.

Purves, Alan C., and Victoria Rippere. *Elements of Writing about a Literary Work: A Study of Response to Literature.* NCTE Research Report, no. 9. Urbana, Illinois: National Council of Teachers of English, 1968.

Rees, Richard D., and Darhl M. Pederson. "A Factorial Determination of Points of View in Poetic Evaluation and Their Relation to Various Determinants." *Psychology Reports* 16 (1965), 31-39.

Richards, I. A. *Practical Criticism.* New York: Harcourt, Brace and World, 1929.

Rigg, Melvin. "The Relationship between Discrimination in Music and Discrimination in Poetry." *Journal of Educational Psychology* 28 (1937), 149-152.

Riggs, Corinne. *Bibliotherapy: An Annotated Bibliography*. Newark, Delaware: International Reading Association, 1968.

Ring, Jerry W. "A Study of the Interpretive Processes Employed by Selected Adolescent Readers of Three Short Stories." Diss. Ohio State University, 1968.

Roberts, Percival R. "An Experimental Study of Selected Effects upon Drawings Produced by College Age Women Using Poetry as Motivation." Diss. Illinois State University, 1968.

Robler, Louise, and M. F. Washburn. "The Affective Values of Articulate Sounds." *American Journal of Psychology* 23 (1912), 579-583.

Rogers, Charlotte D. "Individual Differences in Interpretive Responses to Reading the Short Story at the Eleventh Grade Level." Diss. University of Arizona at Tucson, 1965.

Rohn, Ross W., and Thomas H. Briggs. "Intelligence and Literature." *School and Society* 18 (October 1923), 508-510.

Romney, A. Kimball. "The Kuder Literary Scale as Related to Achievement in College English." *Journal of Applied Psychology* 34 (1950), 40-41.

Rosenblatt, Louise M. *Literature as Exploration*. New York: Noble and Noble, 1968.

————. "The Poem as Event." *College English* 26 (November 1964), 123-128.

————. "Towards a Transactional Theory of Reading." *Journal of Reading Behavior* 1 (Winter 1969), 31-47.

Rosengren, K. E. *Sociological Aspects of the Literary System*. Stockholm, Sweden, 1968.

————. "Litterära Attityder Och Litterärt Beteende." *Litteratur-*

sociologi. Edited by K. E. Rosengren and J. Thavenius. Stockholm, Sweden, 1970.

Ruhlen, Helen V. "Experiment in Testing Appreciation." *English Journal* 25 (1926), 202-209.

Russell, David H. "Contributions of Reading to Personal Development." *Teachers College Record* 61 (May 1960), 435-442.

————. *The Dynamics of Reading.* Edited by Robert Rudell. Waltham, Massachusetts: Ginn Blaisdell, 1970.

Russell, David H., and Caroline Shrodes. "Contributions of Research in Bibliotherapy to the Language Arts Program—I." *School Review* 58 (September 1950), 335-342.

————. "Contributions of Research in Bibliotherapy to the Language Arts Program—II." *School Review* 58 (October 1950), 411-420.

Sano, Katsuo. "College Students' Attitudes toward Literature." *Japanese Journal of Psychology* 20 (1950), 27-32.

Saper, Marshall B. "Bibliotherapy as an Adjunct to Group Therapy." Diss. University of Missouri at Columbia, 1967.

Schneck, Jerome M. "Bibliotherapy for Neuropsychiatric Patients: Report of Two Cases." *Bulletin of the Menninger Clinic* 10 (1946), 18-25.

Schubert, Delwyn G. "The Relationship between Reading Ability and Literary Appreciation." *California Journal of Educational Research* 4 (1953), 201-202.

Scribner, Marion I. "The Responses of Students, Teachers, and Critics to Selected Poetry." Diss. University of California at Berkeley, 1960.

Serling, Albert M. *Three Methods of Testing Literary Comprehension at the Advanced Placement Level.* College Entrance Examination Board Research and Development Board Report 66-7, no. 4. Princeton, New Jersey: Educational Testing Service, TDR 66-2, 1967.

Shirley, Fehl L. "Case Studies of the Influence of Reading on Adolescents." *Research in the Teaching of English* 1 (1969), 30-41.

————. "The Influence of Reading on Adolescents." *Wilson Library Bulletin* 43 (November 1968), 256-260.

————. "Influence of Reading on Concepts, Attitudes and Behavior." *Journal of Reading* 13 (February 1969), 369-372.

————. "The Influence of Reading on the Concepts, Attitudes, and Behavior of Tenth, Eleventh, and Twelfth Grade Students." Diss. University of Arizona, 1966.

Shnayer, Sidney W. "Some Relationships between Reading Interests and Reading Comprehension." Diss. University of California at Berkeley, 1967.

Shrodes, Caroline. "Bibliotherapy: A Theoretical and Clinical Experimental Study." Diss. University of California at Berkeley, 1949.

Skaaret, L. *"God" Och "Dalig" Litteratur: Elever Och Deras Lärare om tva Noveller.* Stockholm, Sweden, 1971.

Skelton, Glen. "A Study of Responses to Selected Poems in the Fourth, Fifth, and Sixth Grades." Diss. University of California at Berkeley, 1968.

Smith, Eugene R., Ralph W. Tyler, and Evaluation Staff. *Appraising and Recording Student Progress. Adventure in American Education,* vol. 3. New York: Harper and Brothers, 1942.

Smith, Johnnie R. "An Analytical Study of the Factors Involved in Learning to Appreciate Literature." *Indiana University School Educational Bulletin* 10 (1933), 47-69.

Smith, Nila B. "Some Effects of Reading on Children." *Elementary English* 25 (May 1948), 271-278.

Snapper, Marion J. "A Study of High School Juniors' Reaction to and Use of Literary Assumptions." Diss. University of California at Berkeley, 1958.

Solomon, Marilyn. "The Relation of Reading Achievement to One Aspect of 'Realism' in Seven-to-Twelve-Year-Old Boys: A Study of the Incidence of 'Moral Realism' (As Conceived by Piaget) in a Sample Population of Retarded Readers and Successful Readers." Diss. New York University, 1967.

Speer, R. K. "Measurement of Appreciation in Poetry, Prose, and Art, and Studies in Appreciation." Diss. Teachers College, Columbia University, 1929.

Squire, James R. "The Responses of Adolescents to Literature Involving Selected Experiences of Personal Development." Diss. University of California at Berkeley, 1956.

————. *The Responses of Adolescents While Reading Four Short Stories*. Urbana, Illinois: National Council of Teachers of English, 1964.

Stewart, Naomi. "Attitudes toward Literary Characters as Related to Factors in Personality." Diss. Purdue University, 1944.

————. "Preferences for Literary Characters as Indicators of Personality Characteristics." *American Psychologist* 2 (1947), 268-269.

Stout, Douglas A. "The Responses of College Freshmen to Characters in Four Short Stories." Diss. University of California at Berkeley, 1964.

Strother, George B. "The Role of Muscle Action in Interpretative Reading." *Journal of General Psychology* 41 (1949), 3-20.

Sussams, T. W. "An Inquiry into the Spontaneous Responses of Children to Poetry." *Journal of Education* (London) 65 (May 1933), 274-278.

Swain, Emeliza. "Conscious Thought Processes Used in the Interpretation of Reading Materials." Diss. University of Chicago, 1953.

Swedner, H. "Läsvanor—Nagra Reflexioner Och Empiriska Resultat." *Litteratursociologi*. Edited by K. E. Rosengren and J. Thavenius. Stockholm, Sweden, 1970.

Syracuse University. *Development of a Testing Instrument to Measure Taste and Discrimination in Literature of Upper Elementary Levels*. New York: Syracuse University, 1963.

Taba, Hilda. *With Perspective on Human Relations*. Washington, D.C.: American Council on Education, 1955.

Tatara, Walter T. "Effect of Novels on Ideas about the Scientist." *Journal of Educational Research* 58 (September 1964), 3-9.

Tauran, Rouland H. "The Influences of Reading on the Attitudes of Third Graders toward Eskimos." Diss. University of Maryland, 1967.

Thayer, Lee O., and N. H. Pronko. "Some Psychological Factors in the Reading of Fiction." *Journal of Genetic Psychology* 93 (September 1958), 113-117.

_____. "Factors Affecting Conceptual Perception in Reading." *The Journal of General Psychology* 61 (1959), 51-59.

Tomkins, Muriel W. "Testing in English Literature: Toward a Better Rationale." *McGill Journal of Education* (Canada) 3 (Spring 1968), 46-55.

Townsend, A. "Books as Therapy." *Reading Teacher* 17 (November 1963), 121-122.

Ulisto, Ingrid P. "An Empirical Investigation of Early Reading Responses of Young Children." Diss. University of Michigan, 1966.

Valentine, C. W. *The Experimental Psychology of Beauty*. London: Methuen, 1962.

————. "The Function of Images in the Appreciation of Poetry." *British Journal of Psychology* 14 (October 1923), 164-191.

————. *Psychology and Its Bearing on Education.* London: Methuen, 1960.

Veley, Charles A. "Literature and the Emotions: A Psychology of Literary Response." Diss. Pennsylvania State University, 1970.

Vergara, Allys D. "A Critical Study of a Group of College Women's Responses to Poetry." *Teachers College Contributions to Education,* no. 923. New York: Bureau of Publications, Teachers College, Columbia University, 1946.

Vine, Harold A., Jr. "Affective Understanding and the Reading of Poetry." Diss. Syracuse University, 1970.

Waples, Douglas, Bernard Berelson, and Franklin R. Bradshaw. *What Reading Does to People.* Chicago, Illinois: University of Chicago Press, 1940.

Weekes, Blanche E. "The Influence of Meaning on Children's Choices of Poetry." *Teachers College Contributions to Education,* no. 354. New York: Bureau of Publications, Teachers College, Columbia University, 1929.

Weisgerber, Charles A. "Accuracy in Judging Emotional Expressions as Related to Understanding of Literature." *Journal of Social Psychology* 46 (1957), 253-258.

Wheeler, Olive A. "An Analysis of Literary Appreciation." *British Journal of Psychology* 13 (January 1923), 229-242.

White, Verna. "Measuring Achievement in High School English." *School Review* 55 (1947), 474-483.

Whitman, Robert S. "Significant Reading Experiences of Superior English Students." *Illinois English Bulletin* 51 (February 1964), 1-24.

Williams, E. D., L. Winter, and J. M. Woods. "Tests of Literary

Appreciation." *British Journal of Educational Psychology* 8 (1938), 265-284.

Wilson, J. W. "Treatment of an Attitudinal Pathosis by Bibliotherapy: A Case Study." *Journal of Clinical Psychology* 7 (October 1951), 345-351.

Wilson, James Robert. "Responses of College Freshmen to Three Novels." Diss. University of California at Berkeley, 1963.

_____. *Responses of College Freshmen to Three Novels.* NCTE Research Report, no. 7. Urbana, Illinois: National Council of Teachers of English, 1966.

Wilson, Robert N. "Literary Experience and Personality." *Journal of Aesthetics and Literary Criticism* 15 (1956), 47-57.

Witzig, James S. "A Study of the Comparative Effect on Retention of Mythological and Factual Prose." *Journal of General Psychology* 55 (October 1956), 173-187.

Wolf, Willavene, et al. "Critical Reading Ability of Elementary School Children." Report. Ohio State University, 1966.

Wolfenstein, Martha. "The Impact of a Children's Story on Mothers and Children." *Monographs for Research in Child Development* 30 (1946).

Wollner, Mary H. B. "Children's Voluntary Reading as an Expression of Individuality." *Teachers College Contributions to Education,* no. 944. New York: Bureau of Publications, Teachers College, Columbia University, 1949.

Wyatt, Nita M. "A Study of the Relationship of Extensive Reading to Certain Writing Skills of a Selected Group of Sixth Grade Children." Diss. University of Kansas, 1960.

Yarlott, G., and W. S. Harpin. "1000 Responses to English Literature (1)." *Educational Research* 13 (November 1970), 3-11.

_____. "1000 Responses to English Literature (2)." *Educational Research* 13 (February 1971), 87-97.

Young, Eleanor C. "The Effect of Intensive Reading on Attitude Change." *French Review* 36 (May 1963), 629-632.

Zaccaria, Joseph S., and Harold A. Moses. *Facilitating Human Development Through Reading: The Use of Bibliotherapy in Teaching and Counselling.* Champaign, Illinois: Stipes, 1968.

Zais, Robert. "A Scale to Measure Sophistication of Reading Interests." *Journal of Reading* 12 (1969), 273-276.

Studies of Reading Interests

Two excellent recent reviews of reading interests, by McKay (1968) and Mott (1970), provide a historical perspective on developments in the research on reading interests. This summary, therefore, seeks to explore methodology and findings. The studies on reading interests are discussed according to the outline below. Many of the larger studies straddle these categories:

Methodology.

The interests: interests in content, interests in form, amount of reading and interests, book difficulty and interests, and literary quality and interests.

Personal determinants of interests: age, sex, intelligence, reading ability, attitude, and psychological needs.

Institutional determinants of interests: availability of books, socioeconomic and ethnic determinants, peer, parent, and teacher influences, and television and movies as determinants.

A. Methodology

A variety of different methods have been used to assess reading interests and study their determinants. Most of these methods are plagued with the usual problems of descriptive or survey research. Problems in reading interests methodology are discussed by Meckel (1946), Braddock (1956), Norvell (1958), McKay (1968), Mott (1970), and, perhaps the most thorough, Lehtovaara and Saarinen (1964).

Differences in methodology, in addition to differences in type and size of population samples, make it difficult to compare results and thereby generalize about interests. Studies often fail to specify procedures employed. Many early studies lacked the methodological and statistical sophistication of later studies. Many studies focus primarily on *what* the interests are by means of checklists, library withdrawals, reading inventories, or questionnaires, while others have explored *causes* of interest patterns by means of case-study methods or measurements which compare the effects of different variables and the relations of these variables to each other. Generalizing about data from different studies is also difficult because of varying assumptions about interests: some studies assume that interests are synonymous with what people read, while others assume that interests are needs, value orientations, positive attitudes or personality traits (Getzels, 1956). Often a clear definition of "interest" is not provided, or certain categories—fiction, non-fiction, reader, nonreader, etc.—are only vaguely defined.

Most studies have repeatedly treated the data in terms of traditional categories, such as age, sex, intelligence, socioeconomic factors, reading ability, and education, rather than considering them in terms of symbolic interaction variables—how the meaning of certain works in certain contexts affects interests (Meckel, 1946).

The most basic problem in methodology is that the instruments used may bias the results. A review of the various measuring techniques suggests that while all of them lack reliability and many lack validity, some may provide information more appropriate for an investigator's particular needs than others.

The most popular device has been the questionnaire. McKay (1968) surveyed studies since 1900 and found that the questionnaire was used two to one over rating lists and two and one-half to one over observation. Questionnaires are used to ask subjects to list or rank order preferred titles or types, to give reasons for preferences, or to provide background information. A more recent technique involves responses to a series of statements about the subject's reaction or attitude toward reading. Stevenson (1969) used a Q-sort instrument of forty-four cards about reading interests and found them to be reliable over a long period of time. An obvious advantage of the questionnaire is that the investigator may direct questions toward particular areas which interest him. The questionnaire depends for its reliability, however, on the subject's ability to comprehend his own motives for reading and on his subjective recall. Subjects may recall only unique, unusual books or books recently read, or they may project their present interests into the past, thus biasing their recall of previous reading (Meckel, 1946). Students may respond in ways that teachers or investigators expect them to respond; their choices may have been directed by what the school or family has provided. Students may be unable to analyze their own impressions of books and to express these impressions adequately. This is especially true of younger students, although Norvell (1958) found high correlations between third graders' questionnaire responses and checklist responses. Despite these major drawbacks, the questionnaire continues to be a popular instrument, especially in teacher-directed research in the classroom.

The interview technique may augment the use of questionnaires in that the investigator can check for biases in questionnaire data. In-depth interviews (Gray and Munroe, 1929; Strang, 1942; Ennis, 1965) can reveal certain personality factors and attitudes, in addition to information about home environment. But the interview technique is time-consuming and requires highly trained investigators.

Another problem with the interview technique is that subjects may not provide accurate information. Shatler (1951) found that students overestimated the amount of reading they did. Preferences stated in interviews may yield different interests than those gained by actual observation, because students may state only culturally approved interests (Byers, 1964). Ennis (1965), however, found on the basis of quantitative data that adult subjects can accurately differentiate between amounts and titles read and their interests, suggesting that older subjects may provide more accurate information than younger subjects in interviews. Ennis used checklists of titles because he found that, although subjects have difficulty in recalling titles, once the title is recalled subjects are able to remember much about the book. Checklists of book titles provide specific information not only about what particular books have or have not been read but also about interests as measured by rating scales. For example, Norvell (1950) used a rating scale of "very interesting," "fairly interesting," and "uninteresting." The formula for the "interest score" of a particular book was the number of students reporting a selection "very interesting" added to half the number who reported it "fairly interesting," divided by the total of all student reports.

When composed of titles assumed to be popular, however, the checklist may not be sampling all the subjects' actual reading. Moreover, subjects may rate books which they have not read.

Thorndike (1941), who noted that brighter students read more and had easier access to books, attempted to minimize factors of actual reading experience by devising the fictitious-titles checklist. Fictitious titles and short annotations describing the content of the book can be developed on the basis of the types of reading under investigation—for example, mystery might be represented by *The Secret Passageway*, with an appropriate description. One problem is that the types or categories represented may not be clearly distinguished by either the investigator or the subject. The subjects may also misinterpret the type due to connotations or identification of the title with actual titles. Much of the success of this technique depends upon what the subjects infer about topics of interest from the titles. Zais (1969) developed the "sophistication of reading interest scale" using paired comparisons of fictitious story synopses instead of annotated titles with secondary school students. This scale represents an advance in measurement technique in that it combines the paired comparison, which has been shown to be highly accurate (Lehtovaara and Saarinen, 1964), with fictitious items. Zais assumed that directionality, or growth in interests, can be measured: the least sophisticated synopses emphasized plot, hackneyed devices, conflict, and stereotyped characters; the moderately sophisticated emphasized characters, character's point of view, some psychological conflict, and ideas of limited scope; the most sophisticated emphasized ideas or theme, a philosophy of life, psychological conflict, and symbolic characterization. Such levels contain certain questionable value orientations toward measuring growth, although the scale was not designed as a definitive measure of growth. Comparison between a teacher-ranking of student interests in four classes and results from the scale indicated no significant differences between teacher assessment and the scale for two classes and significant differences for the other two classes.

A common device in classroom research and in individualized reading programs is the reading record kept by students or teachers. This record does provide information about actual reading, but often the reading is not reported fully. The record may reflect certain reading patterns as determined by the nature of the books available rather than by reading interests (Meckel, 1946). A similar source of information is library withdrawal records, which do reflect some degree of effort as an expression of interests. However, various selectivity factors seriously bias any results: the socioeconomic class of subjects who frequent the library results in a selected sample; libraries may not have additional copies of popular books, reducing their availability; subjects may be more attracted by the size or appearance of the book than by content; the most serious drawback is that the books may never be read, although the withdrawal itself may reflect some interest pattern. These liabilities may be offset by requesting further information from the borrower when he returns the book.

Another technique which is used occasionally involves subjects' ratings of text samples (Dunn, 1921; Gates, 1930; Kangley, 1930).

This method gives the subject a concrete and fresh image of types of reading in a more direct manner than the fictitious-titles (with synopses) checklists (Lehtovaara and Saarinen, 1964). Droney, Cucchiara, and Scipione (1953) found that students selected stories on the basis of content rather than titles. The essential problem with this approach is that a sample of a book may not reflect certain qualities of the whole book, for example, a suspenseful plot. Another problem is whether the sample represents the types being tested. On the other hand, one bias in research has been that interests have been inferred from preferences for titles. This approach could be used to measure interests in certain types of styles, literary devices, or basic genre forms.

The rating scale measurement employed in these various approaches may fail to reflect certain subjective qualities of preference. The free response measurement, as used by Richards (1929), Malchow (1937), and Strang (1942), does allow for unstructured expression of interests but may require careful content analyses to discern specific preference patterns. The free-response technique may contain certain biases toward verbal ability but may avoid biases toward expression of interests in written form if responses are oral (oral responses beget other problems). Content analysis techniques, when applied to those selections which subjects prefer, reveal certain types of content and form (Jordan, 1921; Zeller, 1941). No sophisticated content analysis schema for accurately measuring interests has been devised.

Distrust of self-report techniques has led to recent interest in direct observation techniques, such as noting which book on a table may be chosen by subjects. The assumption behind this technique is that observed behavior reflects interest. Another recent development has been the use of the semantic differential test to measure interests (Klein, 1968).

Little research has been devoted to which of these techniques, if any, provides a more accurate measure of reading interests. Thus, different techniques may have produced such different results that any generalization about results from different studies is highly suspect. For example, Byers (1964) taped topics discussed by first graders in a group free-discussion period. Smith (1962) kept records of first graders' free-choice library selections. Byers (1966) found that science and nature were first-choice topics, while Smith found that humor and fantasy were first-choice topics. Of course, students' interests as reflected in discussions may be quite different from those reflected in library selections.

Only two studies have tested the merits of different techniques. Lehtovaara and Saarinen (1964) compared results from four different methods: questionnaire, fictitious-title booklist, text sample, and paired comparisons. Two thousand Finnish students, ages ten through sixteen, comprised the sample. Twenty-six categories of types of reading were used as a basis for comparison. The booklist and the text samples had the closest correspondence; the booklist and the questionnaire, the next closest. These three methods, excluding the paired comparisons, were relatively similar, although differences in frequencies of the rating alternatives prevented any exact combination. The questionnaire resulted in more suggestive ratings than the other methods. Kiser (1968) studied the effectiveness of measuring elementary school students' attitudes toward reading using the *San Diego County Inventory of Reading Attitude,* consisting of 25 attitude items such as "Do you like to read before you go to bed?" (Howes, 1963), peer ratings, teacher ratings, and verbal achievement tests. The attitude inventory was more effective for boys than for girls in grades three through six; scores from the other three indicators were higher for girls than boys. Although this study was concerned more with general attitude than with interests, it does suggest that certain techniques may be more appropriate for certain groups according to sex, age, ability, or socioeconomic factors. But, if any future synthesis of results from studies is to be achieved, consistent use of one or two techniques is essential.

Another methodological problem with many reading interest

studies is the small reliability due to the small size of the sample. Using a formula for the standard deviation of a per cent $\left[\sigma_p = \sqrt{(p9/N)} \right]$, Norvell (1958) found that samples of 500-1000 subjects in each grade are reliable, but that samples below 300 are questionable. Of course, some investigators may not be seeking quantitative results; in many cases the need to quantify has led researchers away from much subjective data about interests revealed in case studies.

Of methodologies for determining reading interest, then, we may say that observation of books read is the most accurate and the most difficult to manipulate, save in controlled settings. Of the measures which ask for the subject's recall, some form of checklist or questionnaire is better than an open-response question ("What do you like to read?"). A questionnaire which uses some checklist (actual or fictitious titles or descriptions) is probably the best, even though it risks suggesting to the respondent what sorts of things the researcher would like him to read. If we are to pursue the topic of reading interest, then, the construction and validation of a questionnaire format is an important first step.

B. The Interests

This section reviews reading interests in terms of two categories: (1) content or type of subject matter and (2) form-genre types and types of literary devices. (Specific title preferences will not be included in detail in this review.) The content-form distinction has always been an arbitrary one, but one which allows for distinctions between interest types. For example, while interest in form (the novel, suspenseful plots, sensuous style, etc.) may remain constant through a subject's life, his interest in content may undergo changes (e.g., his interest in animal stories or fairy tales may decline rapidly at an early age and may be replaced by interest in sports or mystery). Research on the determinants for interests will be discussed in a later section.

Content

Most research has indicated that content serves as the most important criterion for interest choices (Rankin, 1941; Norvell, 1950; Whitman, 1964). Studies of elementary and, to a lesser extent, of secondary students' interests in content have shown relatively high agreement over the decades. This agreement may result from the consistent use of similar categories in these studies. Certain titles may have fallen easily into set categories, so that the categories were not questioned. Further, content is much too loosely defined. *Adventure* as a category may have a number of interpretations (action, suspense, violence, faraway places, manliness), and the researcher's conception of adventure may be far from the respondents' and one respondent's from another's. There has been no checking of the reliability of a category that we could find. A selection may be classified as an animal story but may have been chosen for its conversation (Austin, 1956).

Another bias of many studies of content is that the researchers never quite freed themselves from notions of what students' interests "should be." Thus, certain subject matter (such as sex or drugs) has been totally ignored. Yet the value of many of these studies is that they do reveal what may be assumed to be students' actual interests, interests which conflict with literature curricula in the schools. Such findings should not remain ignored.

The studies are presented here by age groups—elementary, secondary, and college/adult—in order that certain developmental patterns may be outlined.

Elementary. Many studies recognize similar developmental patterns for elementary school students. A typical list of elementary students' interests has been compiled by Broening (1934): (in order of decreasing interest) adventure, fairy tales, making things, humor, biography, true-event stories, and animals. However, certain rapid changes (more rapid than at the secondary level) do occur. Pupils in the first and second grades prefer subject matter about animals, nature, fantasy (fairy tales), and characters as children (Witty, Coomer, and McBean, 1946; Nelson, 1966; Consuelo, 1967). Students in third and fourth grades become more interested in adventure, daily life or familiar experiences, nature, and animals, with a decreasing interest in fantasy, usually in the form of fables (Curley, 1928). A stronger interest in more realistic subject matter develops as students begin to read more on their own and begin to perceive reading as a source of information about the world (Terman and Lima, 1931). In grades five and six, reading interests become more fixed (Terman and Lima). Adventure is still popular, especially selections with main characters who fulfill students' hero worship; for boys, interest increases in war, travel, and mystery, all of which emphasize the suspenseful or the unknown (Row, 1968); for girls, interest in animal stories, westerns, and fairy tales decreases as interest in love stories begins and as sex differences become more pronounced (Shores, 1954).

Developmental shifts vary with students' sophistication. Thorndike (1941) found that more intelligent students lost interest in less sophisticated content (animals, foreign children, magic, and fantasy) at an earlier age. For older children, bright students lost interest in adventure, school stories, and mystery and detective stories earlier than average or below average students. Little change occurred in travel and adult adventure. Interest increased in school stories and romance for low-IQ girls and in sports stories for low-IQ boys.

Several studies have found shifts in these content preferences since 1900, shifts which might be termed cultural. For example, interest in stories about exotic foreign lands has decreased while interest in stories about space travel or sports heroes has increased. Nelson (1966) compared poetry preferences of students in 1965 with poems in readers of 1928 and found significant differences in content. However, while the content as presented in readers has changed drastically due to changes in educational philosophy and attitudes toward teaching classical literature, many studies indicate highly similar interests over the years and the consistency of children's basic psychological needs—the need to fantasize, explore, or identify with animals, heroes, and children who provide optimistic models for vicarious experiences.

Secondary. Studies of junior high school students' content preferences are important in that the amount of voluntary literature reading reaches a high point in junior high school, only to decline in the ninth grade, and in that differences between the sexes become apparent both physically and in terms of interest. Seventh and eighth grade girls tend to prefer mystery, romance, animals, religion, career stories, comedy, and biography, while boys tend to prefer science fiction, mystery, adventure, biography, history, animals, and sports. Both, however, show an increasing interest in non-fiction, historical and mystical romance, and works dealing with adolescents (Strang, 1946; Leafe, 1958; Smith and Eno, 1961; Carlsen, 1967). By asking students about the type of story they would have an author write, Smith and Eno also found that students preferred a protagonist who was a student between ages 15 and 19 and who was attractive, intelligent, and physically strong.

McCullough (1936), using a similar technique of asking students to write a letter recommending a book and justifying that choice, found that the most important "interest-rousers" were unusual achievement and heroism and that while girls discussed preferences for romance, they demonstrated little realistic understanding of the subject; Wheeler (1920) had earlier found that half of girls' reading was of series books. Malchow (1937) found that boys preferred characters who were highly clever, could outwit others, and were ambitious, while girls preferred characters who were academically bright, socially successful, and considerate.

Developmental differences at this level do occur, especially differences in emotional maturity and susceptibility to mass media influences, as well as intelligence differences. Novotny (1954) found that low-IQ seventh graders preferred stories of stereotyped westerns and adventure. Soares and Simpson (1967) found that high-IQ students were more interested in love and courtship, and that low-IQ students preferred the theme of success or failure.

These findings dramatize how cultural values and socialization patterns in America heavily influence adolescents' interests. The characters preferred reflect stereotyped sex differences—agressiveness for boys and femininity for girls—especially in earlier studies. Until grade nine, students' interests appear free from pragmatic concerns; their motives for reading literature are largely enjoyment and entertainment, culminating in the junior high school "reading craze." Strang (1946) found that interest in psychology and vocational matters develops from grade nine on.

The content preferences of high school students develop to the level that little difference from most adult preferences can be detected (Terman and Lima, 1931). High school students' reading suggests a broadening and maturing of interests, although some students begin to narrow their interests. The major difference from junior high school interests is that high school students read less juvenile literature and more nonfiction; they read more to satisfy informational needs or academic demands. Another difference is that high school interests reflect the need to define philosophical stances and a value orientation toward social problems. Books which deal with social deprivation, inequality, or discrimination are popular (Carlsen, 1967), particularly those with scapegoat heroes. Main characters representing vocational options are also popular. Whether content preferences are developed more by school-assigned readings than by outside-of-school reading has not been researched, nor has the importance of sex books or books of topical interest like Jerry Rubin's *Do It!*

Witty's findings (1961) are typical. Boys preferred adventure, mystery, humor, and science fiction of mature quality but containing much action, while girls preferred romance, humor, mystery, and career stories. To this finding one can add that, among senior high students, there is increased interest in biography, sports, personal appearance, and homemaking; decreased interest in mystery, humor, and drama; and a shift toward character and realistic stories and toward mature romances with more complex plots, more moral decisions, and deeper character adjustments (Elder and Carpenter, 1928; Brink, 1939; Smith and Eno, 1961). Most of these studies dealt with college-bound students. Since colleges in the late 1800s began publishing booklists of recommended reading, much literature reading of college-bound high school students has been oriented toward these "important works," which, especially on earlier lists, were predominantly classical. The reading interests of non-college-bound students have been largely ignored, under the assumption that there existed no well-defined goal, other than "pleasure," for their reading.

Studies reveal a shift toward reading more contemporary titles in the schools, although whether any drastic shift in interests has occurred since 1900 is difficult to discern. Of course, *title* popularity shifts quickly. Charters (1938) found that of 64 novels popular in 1927 only four remained popular in 1936. Titles preferred in 1924 were by Dickens, Brontë, Shakespeare, Verne, and Twain; in 1965 they were by more recent authors—Fleming, Golding, Hemingway, Orwell, and Shute (Hughes, 1924; W. J. Jones, 1965). Students today reveal a stronger disinterest in traditional high school titles (e.g., *The Scarlet Letter, Great Expectations, Red Badge of Courage*), favoring such titles as *The Catcher in the Rye, 1984*, and *To Kill a Mockingbird* (Gallo, 1968).

Little sophisticated research exists on why specific titles or writers are popular, because the usual procedure is to infer broad interest types from title preferences rather than to scrutinize particular aspects of a work. One study which did analyze twelfth grade preference responses to popular titles found, for example, that *The Catcher in the Rye* filled a need for self-identification and shaping of values, *The Ugly American* and *Atlas Shrugged*, for shaping attitudes. One salient reason for shifts in title popularity is that paperbacks have presented a wider exposure to recent titles than have traditional school literature courses. Paperback book clubs have provided a variety of options. One study found that 80 percent of the books purchased were read and 75 percent of the books were "enjoyable"; an important factor in the book club's success was the teacher's attitude (Algra and Fillbrandt, 1971).

College/Adult. The content preferences of college students and adults have received little attention, primarily because investigators find secondary and elementary schools a more amenable setting for their research, although they could start with analyses of best seller and book club lists, as did Q.D. Leavis.

Two studies of college students' preferences reflect a change in interests which coincides with basic changes in college students' values. George Smith (1946) analyzed library records and student reports of weekly reading at the University of Chicago, 1936-1937. He found that only ten percent of the total reading was voluntary and that most reading was related to course work. Novels with psychological, social, or family topics were popular. Brighter students read more humorous and satiric books, while lower-intelligence groups read novels of "adolescent quality." Gottsdanker and Pidgeon (1969) analyzed student reports of books which most influenced them. Forty percent of the reading was fiction (much not assigned) and one half of that was written after World War II. Social and political commentary and religion comprised 30 percent of the reading, and writers such as Camus, Hesse, Tolkien, and Sartre, who reflect existential concerns, were popular.

Studies of adult content preferences indicate that while a wide variety of types are read, professional and recreational interests tend to narrow the range of interests; changes in adults' interests are as susceptible to cultural shifts as students' interests are to changes in philosophy of literature instruction. In a nationwide survey (Link and Hope, 1946) most preferred types were (in descending order of preference) adventure, war, social problems, history, religion, and mystery. Porcella's (1964) review of reading-interests studies of college-educated adults found that businessmen preferred historical fiction and mysteries—only one-fifth of their reading consisted of serious modern novels. In contrast, librarians preferred modern novels. Foster (1936) found that housewives read twice as many novels of family life as the average unmarried woman. One conclusion might be that profession dictates content preference. However, many other variables are operating: Waples (1932) found no significant positive relationship between subjects of interest for factory workers and subjects about which they read, although, given two books equally readable, more reading was done on the subject of more interest. The most important factors were accessibility and readability, rather than content. Further investigation in adult interests is needed on the interaction of different variables of content, availability, and readability. For example, is the popularity of mysteries due to certain content features or to easy availability? Most of these studies were done before the advent of television, and the interaction of media and preferences bears scrutiny.

As far as the content of literature is concerned, then, we can see that there exist certain developmental trends: from fiction to nonfiction, from plot-dominated to character-dominated works, from evident fantasy (fairy tale and animal play) to implicit fantasy (adventure, mystery, and romance). We can see that there are sex differences in reading interests, particularly in the middle grades of school. From this information, teachers and curriculum makers may plan the types of works to offer students. From information about content aspects (character, theme, and the like), they may make some plans for questions and activities. But there remains a need for more detailed research into the substructures of content (incident, character type, and topic), into the developmental pattern within an individual either during the course of reading one work or over the years.

Further, the definition of content has been superficial at best. No one has looked at preferences in terms of plot-types or archetypes. For example, do students prefer stories about fantasy worlds or about the real world? Why does content serve as a more important criterion for interest than form, or are the two always separate in the minds of students? What the questions imply is the need for more detailed content analysis not only of the works preferred but also of the subjects' discussions of their interests. Another promising technique which can be used by teachers is the *Northwestern University Interest Inventory* (Witty, Sizemore, Coomer, Kruppner, and Kinsella, 1960). In this informal child-study approach, teachers and students discuss favorite leisure activities, hobbies, play preferences, and habits related to television, radio, and movies, in addition to reading interests. Thus, some understanding can be gained of how content interests overlap, regardless of activity, and how other activities, especially watching television, affect reading interests. From these understandings could emerge better text selection and a better understanding of teaching strategy to insure the continuation of interest.

Form

The focus of this section is on interests in types of literary forms—fiction, poetry, drama, satire, etc.—and interests in literary devices—style, plot structure, symbolization, etc. The usual procedure has been to infer from title preferences or questionnaire responses that fiction is preferred over nonfiction, e.g., or drama over poetry. Few studies have probed beyond these categories to discern how particular aspects of form affect interest in that genre.

Elementary. Some 25 studies, dated as early as 1899, agree that early elementary students prefer literary to nonliterary presentations. Whether the form happens to be fiction, drama, or poetry is less important than the fact that the presentation is not informational in character. Wissler (1899) suggested that students enter school with an interest in the story form. Narrative material, particularly that with a suspenseful plot, much action, humor, and nonsense is preferred. More detailed studies correlated judges' rating of types of forms present in reading materials with students' interest ranking. Although the categories were not well defined, surprise, action plot, narrativeness, liveliness, conversation, animalness, and moralness were the most interesting to students in grades one through three. Liveliness and moralness seemed less popular, and action and plot, most popular (Dunn, 1921; Gates, 1930; Zeller, 1941). A much more recent study confirmed these earlier ones, adding only the preferred categories of unusual experiences, fantasy, and humor (Stanchfield, 1968). It further showed first graders disliking sadness, family love, anger, cruelty, and familiar experiences, the last a contradiction of some earlier studies, particularly that of Peltola (1963), who found that unusual characters and extraordinary events are unpopular with slightly older children. "Children cannot understand ambiguities and mishaps based on experiences they have not yet had" (Austin, 1956). This should be amended to read "*some* children," for we are not sure at what point children begin to prefer more realistic treatments to fantasy treatments (if they do). Preference for realistic literature may derive from the desire for information, although Shores (1954) implies that a reader's "informational needs" are different from his needs for reading literature. Contradictory evidence on realistic versus fantasy interests is suggested by Nila Smith (1926) who found that realistic stories had a higher appeal than nursery rhymes for first graders and concluded that informational needs were more important than entertainment needs of children who may have outgrown the nursery rhymes. Peltola (1965) found that, of 3,176 boys and girls in fourth and sixth grades, more chose stories classified as "real" than stories classified as "make believe." However, more fourth grade children than sixth grade children chose "make believe" stories, suggesting a developmental trend from fantasy interests to interest in real-life stories or possibly in realistic treatments. Perhaps further research will indicate a complementary need for both forms, and the context of the question-asking may be crucial.

The findings do suggest that primary students perceive their reading, for the most part, as entertainment—the more successful the action plot in gripping their attention or making them laugh the more they like it. Another factor is that primary children tend to prefer a form which does not confine them, which allows free extensions of vicarious experience. Bateman (1967) investigated what factors children found humorous. Individuality of humor and slapstick were more humorous than abstract wit, sarcasm, or puns. Comic passages where humor was evoked by an economy of words were preferred to long descriptions. Nonsense in itself was insufficient; it must be accompanied by sound or visual imagery. Other studies indicated that when compared with informative and nonliterary selections, those with characters and/or narrative elements were preferred, even up to sixth grade, although the popularity of myth and legend declines after that point (Bruner, 1929; Gates, 1930; Norvell, 1958). This last finding has not really been used by curriculum makers. Northrop Frye's typology now might generate further studies as to what specific aspects of myth and legend generate interest at certain grade levels.

Although elementary children are less interested in poetry than narrative forms, the research indicates that certain kinds of poetry are more popular than other kinds. One essential problem revealed by the studies has been the misconceptions of adults about children's poetry interests, especially when poetry is perceived as a means of teaching moral lessons. Those poems which retain elements of prose, narrativeness, action, humor, and lack of ambiguity are preferred. Children preferred poems with a clear story line, nonsense, humor, child experiences, and minimal descriptions; they rejected sentimental, didactic, subtle, and clever poetry, particularly poems with much figurative language and distasteful or disturbing experiences. Length was an irrelevant factor (Kyte, 1947; Nelson, 1966; Pittman, 1966). Although older elementary students tend to lose interest in poetry altogether, their preferences are for poetry with elements of rhyme, emotional tone, and story line, and they especially dislike poems which involve complex sentence structure and highly figurative language (Weekes, 1929; Avegno, 1956; Norvell, 1958). If all this implies a formula for writing popular children's poetry, the poet should remember that content is a more important variable than form.

The studies of stylistic features and appeal to elementary students pose a problem of how style may be defined in more objective terms than is evident in the research. In an early study, Ballard (1914) rewrote a passage according to four different styles: "antique," "florid," "plain," and "jocular." A fondness for the "florid" style (highly dramatic descriptions) increased with age up to adolescence; the "jocular" style was preferred by older students. Students tended to let their interest in subject matter bias their style preferences. Jones and Caterette (1963) found that children in grades one through three preferred language which was less redundant but that "style" of lexicon did not affect interest. Weekes (1929) found that figurative language and, to a lesser extent, involved sentence structure obscured meaning for children. A recent development has been the debate over black children's interest in texts written in black dialect as opposed to the so called standard dialect. In a thorough study using the semantic differential as a measure of interest, Wiggins (1971) concluded that all black third and fourth graders studied were significantly more interested in standard English reading materials than in black English materials and that differences in interests toward black and standard English were not significantly affected by theme, sex, grade level, or age. Whether the same conclusions apply for much older or younger students is an important area for further research.

The appearance of books is an important factor in younger children's interests and might be seen as an aspect of style. Books are often rejected because of their appearance (Elder and Carpenter, 1929); for example, books with smaller print may be judged to be more "grown-up." Also, if a student is seeking approval from peers, he may select a book more on the basis of what he thinks is expected of him than what he actually prefers (King, 1967).

Illustrations were found to be a more important factor in appeal for kindergarten students than content, while for older students amount of illustration was irrelevant to interest, and, in fact, pretentious illustration served as a negative factor (Rankin, 1944; Cappa, 1957). Some children prefer fanciful illustrations and photographs, but illustrations which make the content appear real or lifelike, which depict action, and which are in color are preferred (Malter, 1948; Rudisill, 1952; Whipple, 1953; Amsden, 1960).

One recent issue in the publishing of elementary reading books has been the preponderance of illustrations depicting solely white middle-class children and environments. Due to the recency of this question, little research on it exists. Rowland and Hill (1965) prepared materials with identical stories but one set with illustrations of blacks and the other with illustrations of Caucasians. Black and Caucasian students were observed choosing selections. A significantly greater proportion of Caucasian children than blacks selected materials illustrated with their own race; blacks' choices were more ambivalent. McEwin (1971) confirmed these findings using realistic fiction books and third grade black and Caucasian students of low and middle classes in Texas. This evidence suggests that more non-Caucasian illustrations should be included in literature readers, since lack of familiarity may cause these preferences.

Research in form and interest needs more sophisticated linguistic analysis to determine what particular stylistic features are preferred, and more attention should be given to the interaction of text and picture. Vague categories of "figurative language" oversimplify aspects of sentence structure (active versus passive; much embedding versus little embedding) which may govern interests. As psycholinguistics makes further incursions into the field of reading, the result may be more specific ways of amassing evidence about stylistic preferences.

Secondary. The high popularity of fiction continues into the secondary level, although the impact on this age group of increased adult interest in nonfiction in the past decade has not been researched. Most studies have indicated that about 75 percent of voluntary reading consists of fiction and that about 75 percent of the most "significant reading" consists of novels, with high duplication of titles (Vostrovsky, 1899; Thurber, 1905; Jennings, 1929; Reinhardt, 1930; Center and Persons, 1936; Eberhart, 1939; McCarty, 1950; Norvell, 1950; Andrew and Easley, 1959; Whitman, 1964; Gallo, 1968). These general categories require further breakdown and explanation. In a study of 4,250 junior high school students' ratings of 862 short stories, Simpson and Soares (1965) analyzed responses for aspects of form and content. Together with Zeller (1941), Strang (1946), and Cleary (1939), who also made classifications, they found that the appealing stylistic aspects are action (usually physical), conflict and suspense, humor, clear plot (usually a single plot), simple style with concrete and clear language, and characterization. Definiteness of setting is generally unimportant in determining taste. These studies have been continued by such researchers as Ford (1961) and Scott (1947), who noted that "fairly orthodox storytellers who avoid risky experiments" are preferred to psychological and technically experimental writers. Brockman (1959) provided a similar conclusion that the novel form was preferred to other forms, because the novel involved a perspective of unity, defined in terms of "having a central theme." He found that anthologies were disliked, because, he claimed, they lacked this unity, an interesting finding in light of the massive number of anthologies in use. Meckel's (1946) and Squire's (1964) studies seem to bear out Brockman's contention. Studying a similar phenomenon, Rankin (1944) found that the opening paragraphs of preferred books contained "a direct and illuminating approach to the characters and settings of the stories," which served as attention grabbers. She also found, as have other studies, that the Newbery Book Award selections were disliked for didacticism and verbose style. They are also usually more difficult reading than "popular" books.

Secondary students' dislike of poetry runs through most of the studies, but little effort has been devoted to studying which types are disliked in order to provide collections of poems to students which do not totally alienate them. Only one shows the aversion to complexity and didacticism (Kangley, 1938). Because the only context of exposure to poetry for most students is the school, many of their interests are shaped by the anthologized selections they read and by teacher attitudes. Martin (1947) found that while students preferred descriptive, humorous, or exciting narratives and "supernatural" poems equally well, the best-known poems were descriptive. Analysis of seven anthologies used in the school revealed that an average of 63 percent of the poems were descriptive, suggesting that limited exposure to certain types may have influenced interests. Nelms (1967) confirmed Martin's study: narrative poems were more popular than brief lyric poems and masculine interest, realism, and emotional appeal were preferred to a more rational appeal. More contemporary poems were preferred to "classics." More sophisticated readers preferred poems which were more oblique, serious, and complex. That changes in interests by form do occur was found by Wells (1934), who noted that of four types of humor—absurdity, slapstick, satire, and whimsy—interest in satire and whimsy increased in popularity from grades seven through twelve, indicating interest in more sophisticated forms. Types of interests obviously vary with the sophistication of the reader, particularly interest in humor and poetry, as will be discussed in later sections of this review.

In one of the few studies on preferences in style, two stories were rewritten to make them equivalent in readability; one was rewritten in a clear style with direct conversations while the other was rewritten by removing descriptions of action and using dull wording. A significant difference in favor of the clear style was found; IQ and reading ability were not related to differences in interest rating (Berstein, 1955). More refined descriptions of style than those in this study are needed for further research.

College/Adult. While they read a smaller number of books voluntarily than secondary students, college students and adults maintain high interest in fiction. Academic and professional demands, however, require more nonfiction reading. Most studies of college students found that they read about half fiction and half nonfiction as compared with the average of 75 percent fiction for secondary students (Carnovsky, 1936).

Little research has been devoted to college students' interests in form and only sketchy evidence exists: Bell and Sweet (1916) found that for college freshmen plot was the primary consideration in reading interest and that style was irrelevant for boys.

Recent reports from publishing houses indicate a decline in the reading of fiction over the past decade. While the total number of books published in 1970 was double that published in 1961, the total number of fiction titles published each year has remained about the same (cf. *Publisher's Weekly, passim*). Nonetheless, publishers and librarians point to a decline in fiction reading (Singerman), perhaps as a result of recent increased concern with social and political problems (Berstein, 1970) or because television watching has replaced leisure time reading of mysteries and romantic novels and has brought about the virtual disappearance of the western novel.

However, as was demonstrated with content preferences, the wide variations in education, income, profession, or access to books render generalizations about adult reading suspect. For example, in a survey of college graduates' reading habits, Ennis (1965) found that those persons who read frequently read 28 percent of the total fiction read; those who read occasionally, 40 percent of the fiction read; and those who seldom read, 32 percent of the total. These figures, while not an accurate indication of actual interests, suggest that the type of reader and his professional concerns determine what forms he reads.

One future area for research in form preferences is suggested by psychoanalytic studies on literary response (Holland, 1968; Bleich, 1969). They demonstrate that certain forms fulfill certain psychological needs—e.g., fiction, as opposed to nonfiction, allows for introjection of subconscious needs, perhaps resulting in higher interest among certain age groups. A second area is the fluctuation of interest in certain genres—e.g., interest in the western has declined while interest in the short story has increased, as evidenced by increased publication of short stories. Are persons more interested in shorter forms due to time expediency, or does the short story "speak to the times" more accurately?

Amount of Reading

The amount of books read does not necessarily indicate interest either in certain types or in quality of reading. Many "light" novels are read with little interest. One study concluded that when amount of reading by subjects in a case study decreased, quality of reading increased (Thomas, 1933). Often a person's concentration of interest in one area of high quality—reading only serious contemporary poetry, for example— results in a decrease in amount of reading, although many researchers have assumed that increased amount of reading in one type implies an increase of interest in that type, a relationship which in itself has not been established by any careful research. *Amount* is also an ambiguous term; it usually refers to total number of titles, ignoring variations in length. Amount of reading has also been measured in terms of hours devoted to reading, ignoring variations in intensity of attention. While the latter is a difficult factor to measure, it would provide more useful information for showing inferences about interests than does a measure of the hours spent reading. The essential purpose in research on amount has been to chart certain developmental patterns.

Whether or not ages 12-13 represent the "reading peak" is a contested topic in the research, but most of the evidence indicates a steady increase in the amount of reading during the elementary years up to seventh and eighth grades despite the advent of television (Smith, 1907; Gray, 1928; Eberhart, 1939; Mauck and Swenson, 1949; Wickens, 1956; Andrew and Easley, 1959; Witty, Sizemore, Kinsella, Coomer, and Kryz, 1960; McKay, 1968). Terman and Lima (1931) found that students aged 8-10 read an average of 1.5 books a month; 10-12, 2 books; 12-14, 3 books; 14-16, 2.5 books. The drop off after ages 12-13 was related to an increase in outside activities. Brighter students read more and reached the "reading peak" at an earlier age (Cozette, 1929). Despite deviations in findings, the persistence of the "reading peak" suggests that basic adolescent needs are operating, especially for girls, many of whom read a vast amount at this age. A secondary need may be the need for sensory or creative stimulation. Roderick (1967) found that sixth graders who were highly creative (as measured by verbal tests of the *Minnesota Tests of Creative Thinking*) read significantly larger amounts than less creative students. These and similar personal factors correlate more with amount read than does teaching (Eberhart, 1939; Sauls, 1971). Esther Anderson (1948) speculated that the higher amounts at seventh grade may be due to access to library facilities not available to the elementary level.

Some evidence suggests that bright students read more now than in previous decades. Entering freshman girls at the University of Wisconsin in 1929 used to read an average of five books a year, and freshman boys read three books a year. Squire and Applebee (1968) found students in outstanding American high schools averaging eight books a month. Similar amounts were read by British students (Squire and Applebee, 1969). Other studies, however, have not shown such encouraging results: in 1919, it was found that one-third of high school students read no literature; in 1947, that 38 percent had read none; and in 1967, that 15 percent never read literature and 75 percent had read five novels or less in a previous school year (Willett, 1919; Donahue, 1947; Crocker, 1967).

Most studies of college-student and adult reading indicate that reading is by no means the great American pastime. Forty percent of the men at one college could not recall a title read in the previous six-month period (Jones, 1950). Clark (1956) found that 36 percent of the freshmen and 60 percent of the seniors were "too busy" for leisure reading. Seniors read less fiction and within a narrower range of fiction than freshmen. Half of the college students in one study devoted less than four hours per week (six hours in another study) to leisure reading (Chapin, 1951; Logan, 1972).

Likewise, adults read little, but a small minority read a large amount: 20 percent of all the readers account for 70 percent of the books read, and education is a strong determinant of that 20 percent (Link and Hope, 1946; Ennis, 1965). A survey by the National Opinion Research Center in 1965 (McElroy, 1968) found that half of the adults sampled had not read a book in the previous six-month period. The variety of reading increased sharply with amount read; variety was positively related to amount of education; early and consistent reading increased variety; the amount of reading increased with income; and only one-third of the retired people who were questioned were readers. Their findings are confirmed by several studies (Gallup Poll, 1958-1969; Eller, 1959; Hoar, 1960).

The low status of reading (as defined in terms of who reads how much) involves priorities in deciding what to do with leisure time. The effort expended on reading depends not only upon the existence of reading skills, which correlates with the amount of education, but also upon the intrinsic and extrinsic rewards gained from reading. To quote Asheim (1956), "So long as the reading skill is not highly developed in the majority of our population, it is foolish to imagine a majority audience reading widely and seriously. As higher education becomes more and more the possession of the average man, an increase in serious reading may be expected, but not in a one-to-one relationship. For even when a man can read and has reading materials readily available, he does not necessarily read if the rewards of reading are not apparent to him." Before adults develop reading interests, they need certain reading skills. However, in order to develop these reading skills, a motivating interest is necessary—an apparently vicious circle for educators interested in improving adult reading.

Book Difficulty

Studies on the relationship between interest and the difficulty of a book, defined in terms of various "readability" formulas or more subjective ratings, have ordinarily been used for deciding grade level placement of books. Often, biases about what students "should read," defined in terms of literary prestige, prevent investigators from making a realistic assessment of a work's difficulty.

Shnayer (1969) challenged the need for readability formulas. Based on his findings that high interest significantly enhanced comprehension and low interest increased difficulty in comprehension, he recommended improvement in interest measures rather than in readability. Strang (1946) had noted that readability formulae then did not include interest factors, but Flesch added these factors in deriving his formula.

In the study which generated the *Winnetka Graded Book List* (Washburne and Vogel, 1926), students were asked to read books either too easy or too difficult by two or more years. Interest increased as books became easier and then decreased as they became too easy. When students read voluntarily, they rated books as interesting even when classified several grades higher or lower; required reading resulted in less interest. Clark (1956) found that black college freshmen and seniors preferred books of low difficulty —the mean readability level (Flesch Formula) was ninth grade or below. The assumption that students prefer less difficult reading rests on a reading interest model of tension reduction. The psychological need for challenging stimuli, however, may help some readers find enhanced interest in more difficult material. This may be especially true of those readers who perceive reading in terms of an analytic, literary-critical perspective.

The relationship of reading difficulty to interests of retarded children has received very little investigation. One might expect a relationship between interest and difficulty (Bruning, 1955), but Ridgway (1955) found that when interest in books was high, retarded readers in grades four through eight tended to read above reading levels and tended to complete the book more frequently. The interest in the book influenced the student's estimate of difficulty. The retarded readers studied demonstrated high interest in a wide range of content categories.

Further clarification is needed of the cause and effect relationship between difficulty and interest. When does the reader conceptualize his interest in a book, if he does so at all? A difficult book may seem less difficult to the reader with high interest, but readers may conceptualize the difficulty of a book before ascertaining their interest in it. In other words, does high interest result in ignoring difficulty, or does immediately perceived difficulty deter development of interest in the book?

Further study is also needed on refining concepts of difficulty. Linguistic work in stylistics—sentence complexity, ambiguity, level of abstractness—may contribute to understanding a reader's perception of difficulty. For example, is low interest in poetry due to the reader's need to translate complex embedding or transformations into his own vocabulary? Likewise, are complex plot or intellectual theme related to assessment of difficulty?

Literary Quality

It is important to define the relationship between quality and difficulty of a work; even though they are related, they are not synonymous concepts. The concept of difficulty has been tied to more exacting measures (readability formulas, etc.), while quality remains an elusive concept.

This review will concentrate on more general aspects of the relationship between interests and quality. Interests, as has been defined, determine the area or content to be read. Taste determines the quality of material to be read within a certain area of interest (Bond and Wagner, 1960). (The research devoted to defining various "levels of appreciation" or taste is reviewed on pages 7-12).

Measures of appreciation, of course, depend on the investigator's definition of the concept *quality*. The most commonly held assumption of teachers has been that students will enhance their appreciation through reading a wide range of literature, receiving teacher or library guidance in formulating selection criteria, learning critical skills, and developing aesthetic perception and motivation for reading. Whether these developments can be induced in the classroom depends in part on whether students develop interest in quality. Many educators argue that interest through self-selection will lead to a desire for more challenging choices and can cite some support (Betzner and Lyman, 1937; Wittick, 1960). Others argue that students lack interest in quality because they lack critical tools. The research suggests that education is the primary factor in developing taste (Broening, 1963). Whether education in general or specific instruction in literature is responsible has not been discerned.

Much more research has been devoted to secondary students' interests in literary quality, because any development that takes place seems to occur at that level, although many students continue to read works of poor quality, for example, series books, through the twelfth grade. Students in suburban towns show more steady progress in maturing than students in other towns, and girls more than boys (Coryell, 1922; Elder and Carpenter, 1929; Cain and Brown, 1932; H. Smith, 1956; Hall and Rairigh, 1964). The ratings of quality are usually made by the researchers, and one might question their judgment. Friedman and Peterson (1957) found that high school senior honors students selected works of high quality to discuss on advanced placement exams, although most of the selections reflected required reading for students and the stringencies of the exam. When Adams (1962) examined only the voluntary reading of fiction magazines by ninth graders, he characterized the interest to be in "sex, sensationalism, and escape from reality." In other words, the kinds of demands traditional literature curriculum selections impose on students may alienate many students' interests. They reject the school's conception of "quality" and either define their own criteria or develop interest in literature which is diametrically opposed to the traditional "quality" books the school prescribes. One study found that Carleton College freshmen's reading during high school had been primarily course selections, and much of it of questionable quality. Of the 300 students, 290 had read *Silas Marner,* while only 75 had read *Moby Dick.* Poetry reading was limited to popular American poets, and standard anthology selections prevailed (Elledge, 1958).

One might also question whether teachers perceive quality and, thus, critically assess textbook selections. Several studies in the 1930s found that public school teachers voluntarily read literature of the same quality as that of the general public (Waples and Tyler, 1931). Whether teacher preparation in literature may have possibly affected the quality of teachers' reading, since these studies were done, we have no way of knowing.

The primary reason for the failure of students to develop interest in reading books of "quality" is that the research indicates no relationship between quality and interests. Nelms (1967) found that the quality of poetry had little relationship to poetry interests, and Evans (1968) found no relationship between judgment of quality, as measured by the *Carroll Prose Appreciation Test,* and two reading interest scores of eleventh graders. A study of library withdrawals indicated that higher quality books (as determined by book reviews) were not necessarily the most widely read (Goldhor, 1959). Although quality rose in direct proportion to amount of education in one study, sex and economic status were also important variables. Readers in the professional ranks showed a sharp increase in reading quality (as defined by researchers drawn from those ranks). The fact that education is directly related to quality of reading is questioned by evidence that many college students and adults read little literature of high quality (Bryne and Hanmon, 1936; Foster, 1936; Clark, 1956; Lingeman 1970).

Whether highly educated adults maintain interest in high quality literature was studied by Gray and Rogers (1956). Adults employed by a mercantile establishment were divided into three groups by level of education (eighth grade, high school, and college). Each adult was rated on a five-step scale of maturity in eighteen aspects of reading. They found that none of the three groups read quality literature. The findings suggested that motivation in going beyond immediate needs or low reading competency is a primary factor in interest in quality literature. Participants in the Great Books program, in their voluntary reading outside the program, read only a small percentage of books which were classified as difficult (National Opinion Research Center, 1957). In his analysis of how readers of quality literature maintain such reading interests, Ennis (1965) found no relationship between the quality or diversity of a person's reading and where he acquires books. Noting that adults establish "linkages" from one book to the next through strong interest in a particular author, type, or subject, and that these "linkages" often result from friends' recommendations, Ennis found that readers who are more surrounded by book-reading friends are more likely to borrow and read books than those who read by themselves. The educated adult may also have high interest in a type not generally considered as "quality," for example, mysteries. Establishing a strong interest in a particular author serves as a shortcut in predicting that other works by that author may reinforce the initial interest. More research is needed on the impact of book reviews, book clubs, availability of books, and personal recommendations in initiating and maintaining these "linkages." A related question is whether development of taste is a function of general social maturity and the desire for social prestige. Answers to these questions as well as to those about the definition of quality should help teachers determine their role as salesmen of good taste.

C. The Personal Determinants of Reading Interests

This section examines the research on characteristics of the individual—age, sex, intelligence, reading ability, attitude, and psychological needs—and the relation of these characteristics to reading interests. These variables have usually been studied in isolation, so that their effects in combination are not understood. Using his sophisticated measure of interests (discussed earlier in this chapter), Zais (1968) found that, for grades nine through twelve, considered in combination, personality variables were not significantly related to sophistication of reading interests, but sex, age, IQ, and reading achievement were. Sex, IQ, and reading achievement, considered singly, were significantly related, but age was not.

Age

The content and forms which are of interest to various age groups are discussed elsewhere. This section expands on how maturity determines changes in interest patterns.

Elementary school students' interests show a definite development by grade level. Researchers have found a close conformity of interests to grade level; children at all ages maintain interest in stories of children their own age. The identification at earlier ages is with fantasy figures, usually animals, who represent childlike experiences, while the more realistic stories popular with older elementary children portray peers undergoing unknown or suspenseful adventures (Terman and Lima, 1931; Witty, Coomer, and McBean, 1946; Row, 1968). These generalizations are not hard and fast, because other studies depict fluctuation in rate of change in interest (Amatora and Edith, 1951; Norvell, 1958; McAulay, 1962; Bridge, 1966). How such diverse findings affect confidence in reading lists recommending works for certain grade levels remains to be seen.

The pace of changing interest patterns slows at the secondary level: seventh and eighth graders express a wider range of interests while eleventh and twelfth graders narrow their interests. The change to adult interests seems to begin in eighth and ninth grades, and the motives for reading shift from reading for entertainment to reading for self-understanding. After age 16, interests do not change considerably, unless drastically affected by education or profession (Strang, 1942; Norvell, 1950; Leafe, 1958; Ennis, 1965; Simpson and Soares, 1967). Evidence points to the clear place of the "junior book" in modern literature.

Sex

Most studies find that sex is the most important determinant of differences in reading interests (Thorndike, 1941; Norvell, 1950; Vaughn, 1963). Girls read more and mature earlier in reading ability, although they are not necessarily more intelligent—cultural influences and sexual maturation seem more to be at work (Elder and Carpenter, 1929; Cain and Brown, 1932; Johnson, 1932; Dunlop, 1950; DeBoer, 1958). Studies done in the 1920s and 1930s found minimal sex differences before age nine, while studies in the 1960s found sex differences at a slightly earlier age; all found significant differences (Belser, 1926; Celestine, 1930; Bridge, 1966; Roderick, 1967; Row, 1968).

One explanation for differences in preference between the sexes in the elementary grades is identification with sex-related characters—a phenomenon also explaining sex differences in literary response studies. Another might be sex-role stereotypes. Peltola (1965) found sharp sex differences for fourth and sixth graders in types of characters preferred; other research on nonfiction interests indicates marked sex differences in biography selection based on the sex of the subject. In a careful study, Klein (1968) measured interests as related to occupation and sex of short story main characters, using both a traditional like-dislike statement scale and thirteen semantic differential scales. Sex-appropriate occupations were rated high in interest by each sex. Boys rated male characters significantly higher than female characters in only the occupation of pilot, while girls rated female characters higher than males in each occupation. Boys and girls reacted to the same character in the same story in distinct ways, although changing the sex of the character did not affect comprehension as measured by a cloze test.

Two studies based on psychoanalytic theory of adult recollection of childhood stories were conducted by Collier and Gaier (1958). Most of the appealing features recalled by women were related to fairy tales which were heard at an average age of 4.7 years. The fairy tales emphasized magic, romance, happy endings, and stereotyped female heroines who thought beauty attracts a male hero. The women recalled hearing fewer stereotyped fiction stories at an average age of 8.9 years, reflecting the early impact of sex-role socialization through fairy tales. In a similar study, males recalled stories with dominant male characters whose success depended upon valor and strength; men's recollections were more reality oriented than women's.

The thesis that female teachers maintain sex differences is questioned by evidence that teacher recommendations are more important for elementary boys' preferences, while authors are more important for girls' choices, and that teachers were more accurate in assessing the reading interests of boys than of girls (Carsley, 1957; Stevenson, 1969).

Sex differences in secondary students' reading interests are most pronounced in junior high school and less so in high school, although high school girls demonstrate earlier interest in fiction; greater enjoyment of mystery stories, novels and literary devices, and literature of introspection; and more frequent reading. Boys demonstrate greater interest in action, detective stories, travel, and science fiction. This may result from the more obvious differences in maturity and attitude toward romance at the junior high age level (Grumette, 1934; Jenkinson, 1940; Taylor and Schneider, 1957; Evans, 1968; Walberg, 1968).

Sex differences are not as evident in adult readers. Adult women used to read more, especially well-educated women and single women, and were more apt to relate their reading to their own experiences (Gray and Munroe, 1929). In his summary of the research, Asheim (1955) noted that men read materials more related to their work and more classic titles, while women read more best selling novels. Whether these findings still hold true when a higher proportion of women is working is another question.

Many of these studies may have failed to accurately test sex differences by using materials which would not emphasize stereotyped role expectations. However, the strong cultural effects on reading interests suggest that not only sex, per se, but also culture is a strong determinant. What is therefore required are comparative studies on an international scale. Another interesting phenomenon is that sex differences have persisted despite the fact that boys and girls are required to read the same books in school.

Intelligence

The relationship between intelligence and reading interests has not been clearly established. One factor rarely confronted in the research is that scores on a verbal IQ test as opposed to a nonverbal IQ test may yield different relationships; a second is the difficulty in using IQ as an index of intelligence. In general, the research indicates that gifted children read higher amounts, mature earlier in their interests, reach the "reading peak" at ages 8-9, rather than 12-13, read over a wider range, read for more informational purposes, buy more books, and prefer humor, complex plots, and moral dilemmas more than students with average or low intelligence. Much of the research also indicates that high- and low-intelligence students by and large have similar reading interests. While these two conclusions may seem contradictory, they suggest that it is the combination of high IQ and high reading ability which is a primary determinant (Terman and Lima, 1931; Thorndike, 1941; Zamchick, 1960; Simpson and Soares, 1967; Zais, 1968). More detailed findings indicate that while high- and low-IQ students are equally capable of appreciating quality, bright students in one study tended to choose literature more on the basis of literary quality, and low-IQ students were more influenced by content and prevalence of familiar experiences. Bright students also rate many poems lower in interest than other students (Huber, 1925; Lazar, 1937; Norvell, 1958).

Low-IQ students may have less definite interest patterns due to a lack of strong self-concept. In a study on students' interests at or above their reading level, Packer (1967) found that students of low IQ and high self-concept selected more books above their reading level than did students of low IQ and low self-concept. Other research indicates that intelligence may become a more important factor at the secondary and adult levels because low-IQ students are involved in more selective school programs and socioeconomic level acts as a root cause (Sterner, 1947). Little developmental research provides any conclusive evidence for this shift.

Retarded readers demonstrated few definite interest patterns in one study (Bruning, 1955), while another study (Gunzburg, 1948) found that there were definite interest patterns and that retarded readers may not need special attention in encouraging interests, although emotional blocks may interfere with enjoyment. Retarded readers are more interested in familiar characters and settings and react negatively to anthologies of stories because their short retention spans make it difficult for them to distinguish characters in different stories. These findings imply that individualized reading methods involving self-selection are appropriate for the retarded reader.

The overall findings also suggest that within one class, despite any homogeneous grouping, interests of bright students will be several years in advance of others, requiring a wide diversity in available titles as opposed to one standard anthology.

Reading Ability

Most of the research indicates that while reading ability does relate to sophistication of interests, it does not directly correlate with interests. The research has not carefully examined the different specific factors of comprehension as related to specific interests. Usually reading tests do not consider the reader's interest in the content of items, which could influence the student's score and result in an underestimate of comprehension.

Much of the research examines the "grade level," or "reading level," of books in relation to interests in those books. Washburne and Vogel (1926) found that books were preferred by students whose reading ability corresponded with that of other students who preferred the same books. This resulted in the *Winnetka Graded Book List* and the use of "grade levels" for recommended books. Packer (1967) studied fourth graders' selections of library books which were at their "independent reading level," defined as books with which students are able to obtain a comprehension score of 85 percent and recognize and pronounce 98 percent of the words. The majority of the students preferred books above their "independent reading level." Several studies found no significant relationships between elementary students' reading ability and interests (Lancaster, 1928; Stanchfield, 1960, 1962). Klein (1968) found that comprehension of superior elementary students was not affected by their preferences for occupational types, but that comprehension for low ability students was significantly higher for preferred sex-typed content, and Ridgway (1955) found similar sorts of relationships. In a study abstracted in this volume, Shnayer (1967) showed that high interests resulted in significantly greater comprehension and enabled students to read beyond their reading ability level. Interest as a factor in comprehension is significantly more important for low comprehension groups than high comprehension groups. For readers at or below reading levels, low interest has a negative effect on comprehension. The results of this study give credence to attempts to enhance reading interests as a means of improving reading skills. It also implies that establishing certain grade levels as a method of assuring the reader that he will not read overly difficult books "puts the cart before the horse."

Recently public concern over alleged inadequacies of many reading programs, especially those in city school systems, has increased. Even before the "Right to Read" furor, Lazar (1952) found that only 14 percent of 50 thousand eighth grade students had at least an eighth grade reading ability. If reading programs for secondary students are to succeed in enhancing comprehension through interest, it should be realized that the two are not clearly related. Although in individual cases there is a positive correlation between interest and comprehension—interest associated both with content and form, especially clarity and pace—the relationship does not extend to ability groups (Harris, 1946; Berstein, 1955; Bruning, 1955; Soares, 1962). Jesson-Dibley, Atthill, and Earl (1960) speculated that students' reading ability affected the range of interests in that students who are rapid readers have more freedom to read widely, while slower readers must be more selective. That students often cite lack of interest in reading as a rationalization for reading comprehension problems suggests more effort be expended in helping students develop more definite self-understanding of their interests.

Attitude

This section will examine the small amount of research on how an attitude toward the work will affect interest in that work. To recall Getzel's distinction, attitude implies merely the readiness to react in a particular direction while interests impel an individual's attention toward a work. Attitude does not necessarily entail interest, but interest does entail an attitude—a student cannot be interested in a book and have no attitude toward the book, but he may have an attitude toward the book without being interested in it. The reason for concern with attitude is that students develop attitudes—positive or negative—toward books, but these attitudes may never develop into any interest in active reading of these books. Many students may have a positive attitude toward contemporary fiction but may never read it.

Attitudes vary with the reader's skill, background, efforts, and peer influences, and thus are unique, personal, and highly unpredictable (Squire, 1958). Needs, such as the need to know, to enjoy, etc., find expression in attitudes; if these needs are fulfilled, the result is usually a positive attitude (needs are discussed in the next section).

Sophisticated attitude scales or the semantic differential have been used only to a limited extent in research related to literature. Whitehead (1956) examined the correlations of various attitudes toward novels—those attitudes related to the student, to his school, and to his teacher as compared with attitudes inherent in the book. If the attitudes of students in different schools reading the same book were found to be similar, then the book was the paramount influence, but if attitudes differed, then the other factors would be considered paramount. Students in fourteen British grammar schools were given a Thurstone-type attitude scale to apply to twelve novels read in class. For ten out of twelve books, differences in sex, age, teacher, and school were unimportant, suggesting that the work itself may be a more important influence on attitude than extrinsic factors. This study did not deal with interests, but it does suggest the need to study the effects on interests of attitudes toward school or teacher. Do various methods of literature instruction engender certain attitudes which affect interests? To what extent do other agencies—the home, the mass media, etc.—instill conflicting attitudes and thus result in the development of different interests?

Psychological Needs

Psychological needs are one of the major determinants of interests—satisfying these needs influences interests. Interests and needs are not synonymous; as Getzels (1956) observes, the same need may find expression in many different interests. Some needs may be subconscious, such as the need for vicarious sexual satisfaction, resulting in interest in pornography. Little research has been devoted to how these subconscious needs influence interests.

Researchers have investigated the following types of needs as they relate to achievement:

    I. Need to develop a self-concept (Strang; Packer).
        A. Need to succeed or excel (Kopel; DeBoer).
        B. Need to learn one's psychological social role (Worley).
        C. Need for a conscience or moral rules (Worley).

    II. Intellectual needs.
        A. Need to relate experiences to concepts (Weekes).
        B. Need for information (Stanchfield; Center and Persons).

    III. Emotional needs.
        A. Need to achieve independence (Worley).
        B. Need to achieve a giving-receiving pattern of affection (Worley).
        C. Need to establish sex role (Worley; Jordan).
        D. Need for escape (Butler; Crow and Crow).
        E. Need for enjoyment (Gallo; Evans).

    IV. Social needs.
        A. Need to relate to social groups (Worley).

    V. Aesthetic needs (Emans and Patyk).

These researchers found the primacy of several of the needs: self-concept (Strang, 1942; Packer, 1967); a driving dependence-independence (Worley, 1967); entertainment (Center and Persons,

1936; Butler, 1956; Rogers and Robinson, 1963; Emans and Patyk, 1967; Gallo, 1968); information (Stanchfield, 1962). No study has examined all of these needs together, so that one must be chary of their claims. Nonetheless, there are some useful findings. Worley concluded that middle class attitudes of independence, honesty, loyalty, and affection for adults tended to predominate over matters of social relationship and sex role behavior and that the stories may not be helping students in their psychological development. One implication of this study is that acculturation influences developmental needs.

The question remains as to whether or not elementary students read to satisfy their developmental needs. Shores (1954) found a closer relationship between what children look up in books and what they ask about than between what they look up and what they read about. Rudman (1955) found that students do not want to ask about the same things that they want to read about, but, in contrast to Shores, they do look up the same things they want to read about. Rudman concluded that children seek specific information in their questions, whereas they read for more general reasons. Students do not often read materials centering on their essential needs (Center and Persons, 1936), suggesting that they may be seeking only entertainment. Perhaps escape is an "essential need" with some children. More research is needed comparing elementary students' motives for reading with the fulfillment of needs through reading.

For secondary students both entertainment needs and social adjustment needs operate, but research done in the 1930s indicated that neither were successfully fulfilled in schools. Much of the reading available to students in schools assumed that they needed stronger ethical and cultural value orientation (Butler, 1956; Crow and Crow, 1962; Howes, 1963; Johnson and Shores, 1963; Emans and Patyk, 1967; Gallo, 1968; but see Davis, 1934; Peterson, 1934). Analysis of junior novels, however, indicated the heaviest emphases of development tasks were on acquiring values and an ethical code;

in comic books the emphasis was on social and aggressive needs (Vandament and Thalman, 1956; Frease, 1961). Vandament and Thalman found that girls expressed more social needs; boys expressed more agressive needs. This study and that of Emans and Patyk (1967) found no relationship between class and needs, countering the common assumption that lower class students have particular reading needs. For those readers who are satisfied by reading, research does indicate some correlates. Hughes and Willis (1965) studied the differences in self-concepts between seventh grade "extended readers," who read high amounts, and students who were academically equivalent but who read less. Extended readers had more positive attitudes toward reading than non-extended readers, and they were more self-confident, identified more with their ideal self, were less dependent on others, and viewed the teachers as more dominant.

Other studies indicate little relationship between needs and interests (Saine, 1950; Weingarten, 1954; Zais, 1970). Burton (1947), who attempted to orient classroom reading around students' personal needs, found that while students were inhibited in discussing such matters in class, they were willing to discuss fictional prototypes who embodied these problems.

Individual needs in reading vary so considerably that any generalization about needs and interests is risky. Although the research indicates that reading may not fulfill certain needs, it does suggest that interests are defined by certain needs. Whether or not the needs are fulfilled by reading is determined in part by the effort required for reading—reading skills, time available, or economic investment. Unless the expectation of reward from reading is high, readers may turn elsewhere in order to satisfy their needs, as Schramm (1955) observed in his study of media.

D. The Institutional Determinants of Reading Interests

Availability of Books

Much of the research in reading interests is biased toward inferences about reading choices students have made, as opposed to choices they would make, if more books were available. Students from homes without many books, whose libraries are inadequate, and who are not provided book options in the classroom may not have developed a wide range of interests. This implies an important distinction between merely giving students books and providing options for students' self-selection. Requiring students for whom books are not readily available to read certain books may still not develop their interests. The research indicates that students are highly self-dependent in exercising preferences. Thus, availability as affecting interests may be conceived from two perspectives, directed availability and free-option availability. Of course, readers do develop interests regardless of availability.

Many books made available to students in school do not interest them, whereas when students select from paperbacks, certain "linkages" develop between types or books by one author (Ennis, 1965; Fader and McNeil, 1968).

Books borrowed from the public library were completed more often than those borrowed from the school library, and books borrowed during free time at school were completed more often than those borrowed during regular school library periods. Students prefer books from the library and book clubs to those given them in class. Being allowed to read at one's own speed, helpful librarians, having the freedom to choose materials, choosing from a greater number of titles, and fulfillment of personal interests were cited as criteria for library use by students (Adams, 1933; Butler, 1956; Karlin, 1962; Miller, 1966; Groff, 1967).

Even if the options are available for self-selection, student choices are affected by a variety of criteria, among them sampling some of the books, content, title, teacher recommendation, illustration, author's name, previous introduction by mass media, and friend's recommendation (Lancaster, 1928; Curran, 1931; Zeligs, 1937; Carsley, 1957).

In his discussion of sources of adult reading, Ennis (1965) noted the problem with any such research—different sources (library, home, school, bookstore) vary considerably according to environment, size, and clientele served, and any general comparison is risky. He found no relationship between the quality or diversity of an adult's reading and the source of the reading. The proportion of heavy readers does not vary with availability. Availability acts more as a negative factor—lack of availability may seriously hamper reading. Ennis found an increase in the proportion of nonreaders in cities where book resources were poor. In locales where libraries were poor, bookstore use increased; but poor bookstores did not result in increased library use. Persons who read more used the library more, and book clubs tended to serve less frequent readers (see also B. Johnson, 1937; Hall and Robinson, 1942; Link and Hope, 1946; McElroy, 1968). Studies have indicated that the low quality and amount of black college students' reading is directly related to the lack of public libraries in their home neighborhoods and that access to books is often a problem for them (Dunlop, 1933; Powell, 1954). But beyond these studies, how certain kinds of sources generate certain interest patterns has not been researched. For example, development of paperback bookstores may have enhanced interest in certain kinds of fiction, often depending upon what publishers predict will sell. The teacher should know more of the sources of his students' reading interests.

Socioeconomic and Ethnic Determinants

Most of the research concludes that socioeconomic factors do not significantly affect interests, that lower, middle, and upper class students have relatively similar interests, although differences in amount and range due to IQ and reading ability do appear. One explanation is that the majority of the studies examined white students who were exposed to a literature curriculum of middle-class orientation. Another is that interest types have usually been inferred from titles known or available to students, which may provide little indication of their actual interests. Moreover, the titles on checklists or questionnaires have not until recently included options of ethnic or minority writers. The type of questionnaire employed may be biased toward verbal ability. As with all research, it is difficult to separate out variables of IQ, reading ability, education, attitudes, or needs from socioeconomic determinants.

Little difference has been found in the interests of rural, suburban, and metropolitan students, although rural students once read less (Weiser and Ashbaugh, 1924; Curran, 1931; Smith, 1941; Hull, 1951; Shores, 1954; Rudman, 1955). Differences in interests, but no significant differences, are due to class, although students in middle and lower classes tend to read more for recreation than for information or aesthetic purposes (Sterner, 1947; Vandament and Thalman, 1956; Wade, 1964; Emans and Patyk, 1967).

The research on ethnic preferences is often devoted to simplistic comparisons between interests of Caucasians and non-Caucasians without dealing in detail with specific types of interests of one group of students or another. Significant differences between interests of black and white elementary and secondary students and adults have emerged, the widest difference occurring at intermediate levels (Gray and Monroe, 1929; Link and Hope, 1946; Gray and Rogers, 1956; Ennis, 1965; Barrett and Barrett, 1966; Olson and Rosen, 1966; Row, 1968; Barchas, 1971). These differences may be due more to Caucasian students' preference for only Caucasian subject matter than black students' intolerance of Caucasian subject matter. Rowland and Hill (1965) and McEwin (1971) found that a significantly greater proportion of Caucasian students preferred materials illustrated with Caucasians while blacks were more ambivalent. Other studies have concluded that ethnic differences did not significantly affect differences in interest (McCloskey, 1966; Ford and Koplyay, 1968; Barchas, 1971). Obviously the fluctuation in results has a great deal to do with the temper of the times; perhaps we cannot at this point know. For example, black kindergarten students in one study strongly favored books about ghetto children; white children disliked them, while black children disliked animal stories (Lewis, 1970). But what were the political and social pressures in the area at the time?

Much more research is urgently needed on what variables (television, home experiences, instructional methods, etc.) have what effect on urban minority interests, particularly in the light of reading problems which have been perpetuated by lack of interest in the classroom materials used. The question of how historical shifts in social values affect interests has not been studied. One investigator, Munson (1944), claimed that high interest in particular writers may be due to the "relevance" of the writer to that particular time (Whitman's patriotism was popular during World War II, etc.), a highly questionable contention. The research indicates more of a gradual shift in interests over the years, especially in terms of sex-role identification, rather than any alteration of interests due to particular social or world events. Studies of nonfiction preferences might find more dramatic shifts in interests over a period of years.

Peer, Parent, and Teacher Influences

Peers, parents, and teachers influence interests directly through recommendations or assigned reading and indirectly by serving as models for emulation. Getzels (1956) argued that the latter influenced interests more effectively than instruction. On the other hand, these influences may be negative in that they may limit interests, or, through prescriptive attempts to impose interests, cause resentment. Gallo (1968) found that teachers and librarians had little influence on student reading preferences because students rarely discussed books with them, although other studies indicate that close to peer recommendation, the teacher's enthusiasm for literature can be an important factor in the development of reading interests (Coast, 1928; Broening, 1934; Carsley, 1957; Cappa, 1958; Woolcock, 1963).

Parents seem to know more about children's reading interests than do teachers and other reading "experts." Numerous studies concluded that teachers misjudged students' interests (Huber, 1926; West and Caldwell, 1933; Norvell, 1958; Johnson and Shores, 1963; Payne, 1963; Nelson, 1966; Nelms, 1967; but see Stevenson, 1969). Two studies have found that parents are able to accurately predict children's reading interests (Shores, 1954; Jefferson, 1956). Seventh graders whose amount of reading was high were found to have parents who read large amounts, were more oriented toward college for their children, and were more satisfied with their children's reading than parents of bright seventh graders whose children read less (Hughes and Willis, 1965).

The research suggests that students should be consulted about their interests more often than at present and experts should be consulted less about grade level placement of reading materials and reading interests.

Television and Movies as Determinants

Research indicates that the effect of the media on behavior in general or reading interests in particular is highly complex and not easily predictable. Whereas reading interests correlate more directly with certain variables, such as education, sex, or reading ability, movie and television viewing draws its audience from all age levels, regardless of certain variables, although certain types of media content are oriented toward specific audiences.

Postman's (1961) review of the research found that only short term effects of television had been studied, so that predicting alteration of basic interest patterns may be premature. Developmental comparison of children's pre- and post-television interests are now impossible.

Students now devote more of their leisure time to television than to reading. In 1959 the order of frequency of exposure to various media for fifth and sixth graders was, from most to least frequent, television, comic strips, books, comic books, radio, and movies (Bailyn, 1959; Miller, 1966). Bailyn found that most students fall into one of two categories in use of leisure time: one group spent its time attending to visual media—television, movies, and comics —and the other group preferred books and radio, implying a more verbal modality. The general lack of correlation between hours of television viewing and hours of voluntary reading tends to support Bailyn's contention that individual differences according to modalities preclude any generalization about kinds of television effects (Hildreth, 1958; Himmelweit, 1958; Stanchfield, 1960), although other studies suggest that film supports reading interest (Witty, 1961; Miller, 1966; Gallo, 1968). However, little research exists concerning the effect of films on interest. One study found that viewing a film of excerpts of a novel generated more interest in the novel than was generated viewing the film version of the entire novel.

The brevity of this section reflects the scarcity of careful research on media effects on reading. The issue of the status of reading in an electronic age requires more sensitive analysis that it has usually been accorded.

The plethora of studies in reading interest has, in sum, been plagued by methodological problems that render many of their finer results dubious, but they do depict some general trends. The interest of students is most closely associated with the content of a work rather than its form or style, and the patterns of interest in content show differences between younger and older children and between boys and girls. The differences are, for the most part, predictable, but individual variation is such that a teacher should beware of stereotyping the interests of students according to age or grade level. The same may be said for predictions concerning style and form, except that we can assert that interest in aesthetic complexity is an acquired taste—whether it is inculcated in school or not is another matter. Most students prefer plain, suspenseful fare. Their preferences for difficult and "renowned" masterworks seem to be inculcated rather than natural concomitants of growing up. The research also indicates the relationship of reading interests to intelligence and to socioeconomic background, but especially to the individual needs of the students. Need perhaps confounds any generalizations, for one cannot assume that any one group is uniform in its psychological makeup. These conclusions being so, and given the seeming lack of impact of the school, the teacher must beware overestimating the power of role and look more deeply at the needs and drives of the students in the classroom. Perhaps some of the methodologies described in the early part of the chapter could be of use here. Certainly, researchers could profitably explore the relationship between needs and other psychological aspects of the individual and reading interests so as to enable the curriculum maker and the teacher to function more effectively.

Bibliography

Abbott, Allen. "Reading Tastes of High School Pupils." *School Review* 10 (October 1902), 585-600.

Abernethy, D., Sheila Ferguson, Yvonne McKay, and F. Thompson. "Children's In-School Reading in Belfast: A Suggested Survey." *Reading* 1 (1967), 10-18.

Abraham, Willard. "The Reading Choices of College Students." *Journal of Educational Research* 45 (Fall 1952), 459-465.

Adams, E. "The Extent of Library Reading in the Junior High School." *School Review* 41 (1933), 375-378.

Adams, J. Q. "A Study of Leisure Time Reading Preferences of Ninth Grade Students." *High School Journal* 46 (1962), 67-72.

Aizerman, L. S. "Contemporary Literature through the Eyes of Upper Grade Students." *Soviet Education* 7 (January 1965), 3-16.

American Library Association. "ALA Report on Major Reading Interests, 1944." *School and Society* 61 (March 1945), 167.

_____. "Change in Readers' Interest." *School Life* 29 (June 1947), 29.

Amatora, Sister May, and Sister Mary Edith. "Children's Interest in Free Reading." *School and Society* 73 (March 3, 1951), 134-137.

Ames, A. C. "Students Grade Authors." *College English* 9 (December 1947), 159-161.

Amsden, Ruth H. "Children's Preferences in Picture Story Book

Variables." *Journal of Educational Research* 53 (April 1960), 309-312.

Anderson, Esther M. "A Study of Leisure Time Reading of Pupils in Junior High School." *Elementary School Journal* 48 (1948), 258-267.

Anderson, H. A. "Objectives for Improving Reading Interests in Grades Ten through Fourteen." *Developing Permanent Interest in Reading.* Supplementary Educational Monographs, no. 84. Edited by H. M. Robinson, pp. 37-41. Chicago, Illinois: University of Chicago Press, 1956.

Anderson, R. E. "A Preliminary Study of the Reading Tastes of High School Pupils." *Pedagogical Seminary* 19 (1912), 438-460.

Anderson, William E. "The Reading Interests of 347 Negro High School Pupils of Dunbar High School, Oknulgee, Oklahoma." Diss. Colorado State College at Greeley, 1943.

Anderson, W. E., and S. L. Crawley. "Reading Interests of Negro High School Pupils." *Quarterly Review of Higher Education among Negroes* 13 (January 1945), 5-11.

Andersson, B. E. *Studies in Adolescent Behavior.* Uppsala, Sweden, 1969.

Andrew, D. C., and C. Easley. "Analyzing Reading Interests." *Clearing House* 33 (1959), 496-501.

Anonymous. "What Do American Children Read?" *The Bookman* 14 (1922), 513-517.

Anonymous. "When Schoolboys Choose Their Books." *Outlook* 131 (1924), 137.

Appleby, Bruce C., and John Conner. "Well, What Did You Think of It?" *English Journal* 54 (1965), 606-612.

Armstrong, Chloe. *Reading Tastes of Waterloo Seniors Applying Linguistics.* Second Yearbook of the Iowa Council of Teachers of English. Urbana, Illinois: National Council of Teachers of English, 1957.

Asheim, Lester. "What Do Adults Read?" *Adult Reading*. Fifty-fifth Yearbook of the National Society for the Study of Education, pp. 5-28. Chicago, Illinois: University of Chicago Press, 1956.

Atkinson, F. W. "The Reading of Young People." *Library Journal* 33 (1908), 129-134.

Austin, Martha L. "A Survey of Current Reading Interests." *Developing Permanent Interest in Reading*. Supplementary Educational Monographs, no. 84. Edited by H. M. Robinson, pp. 53-56. Chicago, Illinois: University of Chicago Press, 1956.

Avegno, Sylvia. "Intermediate-Grade Children's Choices of Poetry." *Elementary English* 33 (November 1956), 428-432.

Bailyn, Lotte. "Mass Media and Children: A Study of Exposure Habits and Cognitive Effects." *Psychological Monographs* 73, no. 1 (1959).

Baker, J. E. "An Analytical Study of the Reading Habits and Accomplishments of High School Pupils." *Elementary School Journal* 28 (1928), 587-602.

Ballard, P. B. "Prose Preferences of School Children." *Journal of Educational Psychology* 5 (1914), 10-21.

Bamberger, Florence E. "The Effect of the Physical Make-Up of a Book upon Children's Selections." *Studies in Education,* no. 4. Baltimore, Maryland: Johns Hopkins University Press, 1922.

Banta, N. K. "An Analytical Study of the Individual Reading of Junior High School Pupils." *Bulletin of the National Association of Secondary School Principals* 13 (1929), 94-96.

Barbe, W. B. "A Study of the Reading of Gifted High School Students." *Educational Administration and Supervision* 38 (1952), 148-154.

———. "Interests and the Teaching of Reading." *Education* 83 (1963), 486-490.

Barchas, Sarah E. "Expressed Reading Interests of Children of Differing Ethnic Groups." Diss. University of Arizona, 1971.

Barrett, C. Patricia and G. V. "Enjoyment of Stories in Terms of Role Identification." *Perceptual and Motor Skills* 23 (1966), 1164.

Bateman, Robin B. "Children and Humorous Literature." *School Librarian and School Library Review* 15 (July 1967), 154-156+.

Beggs, B. B. "Individual Differences in Recreatory Reading." *School Executive* 50 (1931), 554-556, 579.

Beery, A., et al. "Developing the Reading Interests of Children." *Elementary English Review* 20 (1943), 279-286.

Bell, J. C., and I. B. Sweet. "The Reading Interests of High School Pupils." *Journal of Educational Psychology* 7 (1961), 39-45.

Belser, Danzlu. "The Reading Interests of Boys." *Elementary English* 3 (November 1926), 292-296.

Berstein, Margery R. "Relationship between Interest and Reading Comprehension." *Journal of Educational Research* 49 (December 1955), 283-289.

Betzner, J., and R. L. Lyman. "The Development of Reading Interests and Tastes." *The Teaching of Reading: A Second Report.* Thirty-sixth Yearbook of the National Society for the Study of Education, pp. 185-205. Chicago, Illinois: University of Chicago Press, 1937.

Blom, G. E., R. R. Waite, and Sara Zimet. "Content of First Grade Reading Books." *The Reading Teacher* 21 (1968), 317-323.

Blount, Nathan S. "The Effect of Selected Junior Novels and Selected Adult Novels on Student Attitudes toward the 'Ideal' Novel." Diss. Florida State University, 1963.

————. "The Effect of Selected Junior Novels and Selected Adult Novels on Students' Attitudes toward the 'Ideal Novel.'" *Journal of Educational Research* 59 (1965), 179-182.

Bokutredningen. Statens Offentliga Utredningar. Stockholm, Sweden (1952), 23.

Bridge, Ethel B. "Using Children's Choices of and Reactions to Poetry as Determinants in Enriching Literary Experience in the Middle Grades." Diss. Temple University, 1966.

Brink, W. G. "Reading Interests of High School Pupils." *School Review* 47 (1939), 613-621.

Brink, W. G., S. Garfield, and P. Witty. "The Reading Interests of Negro High School Students." *Educational Administration and Supervision* 26 (1940), 607-613.

Brockman, F. J. "Survey of Pupil Interest in Literature." *High Points* 36 (January 1954), 13-16.

Broening, Angela M. "Factors Influencing Pupils' Reading of Library Books." *Elementary English Review* 11 (1934), 155-158.

Brown, Carol L. "A Study of Procedures for Determining Fifth Grade Children's Book Choices." Diss. Ohio State University, 1971.

Brumbaugh, F. N. "Children's Choices of Reading Materials." *Elementary English Review* 16 (October 1939), 226-228.

Bruner, Herbert B. "Determining Basic Reading Materials through a Study of Children's Interests and Adult Judgments." *Teachers College Record* 30 (January 1929), 285-309.

Bruning, Herbert I. "A Study of the Readability, Interest, and Usefulness of Selected Materials for Retarded Readers in Grades 7–12." *Kansas University Bulletin of Education* 10 (1955), 16-23.

Butler, Joan W. "A Study in Adolescent Reading." *Library Association Record* 58 (October 1956), 387-389.

Byers, Loretta. "Pupils' Interests and the Content of Primary Reading Texts." *Reading Teacher* 17 (January 1964), 227-233.

————. "The Interests of Space-Age First Graders." *Elementary School Journal* 64 (1964), 237-241.

Byrns, R., and V. A. Henmon. "Reading Interests of High School Seniors." *English Journal* 25 (1936), 61-64.

Cain, W. R., and F. J. Brown. "An Evaluation of the Outside Reading Interests of a Group of Senior High School Pupils." *Journal of Educational Sociology* 5 (1932), 437-442.

Cappa, Dan. "Kindergarten Children's Spontaneous Responses to Story Books Read by Teachers." *Journal of Educational Research* 52 (October 1958), 75.

Carlsen, G. Robert. *Books and the Teen-Age Reader.* New York: Harper & Row, Publishers, 1967.

Carnovsky, Leon, and Hazel A. Johnson. "Recreational Reading of Graduate Students." *Journal of Higher Education* 8 (January 1936), 7-12.

Carsley, J. D. "The Interests of Children in Books." *British Journal of Educational Psychology* 27 (1957), 13-23.

Center, Stella S., and G. L. Persons. "Leisure Reading of New York City High School Students." *English Journal* 25 (November 1936), 717-726.

Chamberlain, Essie. "Literary Attitudes and Reactions of Boys and Girls." *Illinois Association of Teachers of English Bulletin* 13 (January 1921), 1-15.

Chapin, Richard. "The Recreational Reading of University of Illinois Students." *College and Research Libraries* 12 (1951), 155-157.

Charters, W. W. "Sixty-four Popular Boys' Books." *Library Journal* 63 (May 1938), 399-400.

Clark, Geraldine L. "A Comparative Study of the Fictional Reading of Negro College Freshmen and Seniors." Diss. University of Chicago, 1956.

Cleory, Florence D. "Recreational Reading in Junior High School." *Nations Schools* 16 (1935), 31-33.

_____. "Why Children Read." *Wilson Library Bulletin* 14 (October 1939), 119-126.

Coast, Alice B. "Children's Choices in Poetry as Affected by Teachers' Choices." *Elementary English Review* 5 (May 1928), 145-147, 159.

Collier, Mary J., and Eugene L. Gaier. "Adult Reactions to Preferred Children's Stories." *Child Development* 24 (March 1958), 97-103.

_____. "Preferred Childhood Stories of College Women." *American Imago* 15 (Winter 1958), 401-410.

Coryell, H. V. "What Books Do Boys Recommend to Each Other?" *Outlook* 131 (August 1922), 645-646.

Cox, R. M. "The Individual and the Reading Course in a Two-Year Technical High School." *Teachers College Journal* 1 (November 1929), 35-48.

Coxe, W. W. "Scientific Literature of the Reading Interests of School Children." *Library Journal* 57 (1932), 9-15.

Coy, G. L. "The Interests, Abilities, and Achievements of a Special Class of Gifted Children." *Teachers College Contributions to Education*, no. 131. New York: Bureau of Publications, Teachers College, Columbia University, 1923.

Cozette, A. Groves. "A Study of Factors That Influence Independent Reading among High School Pupils." Thesis. University of Chicago, 1929.

Crocker, Oswald K. "The Leisure Reading of High School Students in Newfoundland, Library Facilities in the Schools, and Home Background as Related to Reading." Diss. University of Indiana, 1967.

Crompton, Margaret. "Technique for Describing the Reading Interests of Adults." Thesis. University of Chicago, 1929.

Crow, Charles S. "Evaluation of English Literature in the High School." Diss. Columbia University, 1924.

Crow, L. D. and A. "The Expanding Interests of Adolescents." *High School Journal* 46 (1962), 23-34.

Cruzat, Gwendolyn S. "A Study of the Relationship between the Books Selected by Children Who Patronize the Negro Branches of the Atlanta Public Library." Thesis. Atlanta University, 1954.

Curley, A. M. "An Analysis of the Methods Used in Investigating Children's Interests and a Summary of the Findings." In *The Reading Interests and Habits of Adults*. Edited by W. S. Gray and R. Munroe, pp. 108-110. New York: The Macmillan Company, 1929.

Curran, Helen. "An Analytical Study of the Free Reading of Pupils of Aledo High School." Thesis. University of Chicago, 1931.

Daigon, Arthur. "The Dominant Themes in the Free Reading of Seventh Grade Students in Relation to the Factors of Sex and Reading Comprehension." Diss. New York University, 1962.

Davis, R. A., and H. E. Taylor. "Significance of Research on Interests for the Classroom Teacher." *Educational Administration and Supervision* 29 (1943), 357-369.

Davis, Sada E. "Poetry Interests of Secondary School Students." Thesis. Rutgers University, 1934.

DeBoer, John J. "What Does Research Reveal about Reading and the High School Student?" *English Journal* 47 (May 1958), 271-281.

DeLara, L. E. "What Do Your Pupils Read?" *Nations Schools* 42 (1948), 45-46.

Donahue, Edward. "Leisure Time Reading Interests of Catholic

High School Boys." *Catholic Educational Review* 45 (November 1947), 525-533.

Downen, Thomas W. "Personal Reading Interests as Expressed by Children in Grades Three, Four, and Five in Selected Florida Public Schools." Diss. Florida State University, 1971.

Droney, Margaret L., Stella M. Cucchiara, and Alice M. Scipione. "Pupil Preference for Titles and Stories in Basal Readers for the Intermediate Grades." *Journal of Educational Research* 47 (December 1953), 271-277.

Dunlap, Mollie. "Recreational Reading of Negro College Students." *Journal of Negro Education* 2 (October 1933), 448-459.

Dunlop, Doris C. "Children's Leisure-Reading Interests." *Studies in Reading, Vol. II*. Publications of the Scottish Council for Research in Education, 34, pp. 81-105. London: University of London Press, Ltd., 1950.

Dunn, Fannie W. "Interest Factors in Primary Reading Material." *Teachers College Contributions to Education*, no. 113. New York: Bureau of Publications, Teachers College, Columbia University, 1921.

Dyer, Clara A. "The Assignment of Poems to the Grades." Thesis. University of Chicago, 1926.

Eaton, H. T. "What High School Pupils Like to Read." *Education* 43 (December 1922), 204-209.

Eberhart, Wilfred. "Evaluating the Leisure Reading of High School Pupils." *The School Review* 47 (April 1939), 257-269.

Eckert, Mollie H. "Children's Choices of Poems." *Elementary English Review* 5 (June 1928), 182-185, 192.

Elder, Vera, and H. S. Carpenter. "Reading Interests of High School Children." *Journal of Educational Research* 19 (April 1929), 276-282.

Elledge, Scott. "What Literature Do College-Bound Students Read?" *English Journal* 47 (March 1958), 147-150.

Emans, R., and Gloria Patyk. "Why Do High School Students Read?" *Journal of Reading* 10 (1967), 300-304.

Ennis, Philip. *Adult Book Reading in the United States.* Chicago, Illinois: National Opinion Research Center, 1965.

Erickson, John E. "Developing Tastes in Poetry." Diss. Wayne State University, 1970.

Evans, John L. "Two Aspects of Literary Appreciation among High School Students, Judgment of Prose Quality and Emotional Responses to Literature, and Selected Aspects of Their Reading Interests." Diss. University of Minnesota, 1968.

Feltman, Irene. "Study of Fiction as a Source Material in Vocational Guidance." Diss. University of Illinois, 1954.

Fenton, N. "Reading Interests of Delinquent Boys." *Journal of Juvenile Research* 15 (1931), 28-32.

Fisk, Robert. "A Survey of Leisure Reading in the Junior High Schools of Alberta." Diss. University of Alberta, 1961.

Ford, N. A. "What High School Students Say about Good Books." *English Journal* 50 (1961), 539-545.

Ford, Robin C., and Janos Koplyay. "Children's Story Preferences." *The Reading Teacher* 22 (1968), 232-237.

Forman, Earl. "An Instrument to Evaluate the Literary Appreciation of Adolescents." Diss. University of Illinois, 1951.

Foster, Jeannette H. "An Approach to Fiction through the Characteristics of Readers." *Library Quarterly* 6 (1936), 124-174.

Fox, Maude G. "An Experiment in Promoting Interest in Reading." *Elementary School Journal* 47 (1947), 451-460.

Frank, Josette. "What Are Children Reading in This TV Age?" *Child Study* 34 (Spring 1957), 6.

Frease, Cynthia R. "Mary Stolz, Junior Novelist: An Analysis of the Literary Characteristics and the Concern with the Developmental Tasks of Adolescence in the Stolz Junior Novels, and the Reaction to Them of Professional Critics and Adolescent Girls." Diss. Colorado State College, 1961.

Friedman, Albert B. "The Literary Experience of High School Seniors. *English Journal* 44 (December 1955), 521-554.

Friedman, Albert B., and R. S. Peterson. "The Reading of Superior Students: A Report of the Literature Examination (1955) of the School and College Study of Admission with Advanced Placement." *Illinois English Bulletin* (February 1957), 1-20.

Friedman, K. C., and C. L. Nemzek. "A Survey of Reading Interest Studies." *Education* 57 (1936), 51-56.

Friedson, Eliot. "Adult Discount: An Aspect of Children's Changing Tastes." *Child Development* 24 (1953), 39-49.

Furness, Edna L. "Researches on Reading Interests." *Education* 84 (1963), 3-7.

Gallo, Donald R. "Free Reading and Book Reports—An Informal Survey of Grade Eleven." *Journal of Reading* 11 (1968), 532-538.

"Gallup Opinion Index." *Gallup Poll Report* 47 (May 1969).

Gates, Arthur I. *Interest and Ability in Reading.* New York: The Macmillan Company, 1930.

Getzels, Jacob W. "The Nature of Reading Interests: Psychological Aspects." *Developing Permanent Interest in Reading.* Supplementary Educational Monographs, no. 84. Edited by H. M. Robinson. Chicago, Illinois: University of Chicago Press, 1956.

————. "The Problem of Interests: A Reconsideration." *Reading: Seventy-Five Years of Progress.* Supplementary Educational Monographs, no. 96. Edited by H. Alan Robinson, pp. 97-106. Chicago, Illinois: University of Chicago Press, 1966.

Glenn, Robert J. "Relating the Subcultural World of the Teenager to Literature." Diss. United States International University, 1968.

Goldberg, H. B. "Using Radio and Television to Incite Interest in Reading in Grades 10-14." *Developing Permanent Interest in Reading.* Supplementary Educational Monographs, no. 84. Edited by H. M. Robinson, pp. 105-109. Chicago, Illinois: University of Chicago Press, 1956.

Goldhor, Herbert. "Are the Best Books the Most Read?" *The Library Quarterly* 29 (October 1959), 251-255.

Gordon, L. "Amount and Kind of Recreational Reading Done by Students of Colorado State College of Education." Diss. Colorado State College, 1940.

Gottsdanker, J. S., and E. A. Pidgeon. "Current Reading Tastes of Young Adults." *Journal of Higher Education* 40 (May 1969), 381-385.

Grant, Emma B., and Margaret L. White. "A Study of Children's Choices of Reading Materials." *Teachers College Record* (April 1925), 671-678.

Gray, William S. "Permanent Interest in Reading." *National Education Association Journal* 20 (1931), 137-138.

––––––. "Summary of Reading Investigations, July 1, 1926, to June 30, 1927, III." *Elementary School Journal* 28 (1938), 587-602.

––––––. "The Challenge Faced in Promoting Desirable Reading Interests." *Education* 79 (May 1959), 551-556.

Gray, William S., and R. Munroe. *The Reading Interests and Habits of Adults.* New York: The Macmillan Company, 1929.

Green, J. L. "When Children Read for Fun." *School and Society* 17 (1923), 390-392.

Green, Ward H. "Comprehension in High School Literature." *English Journal* 15 (December 1926), 765-772.

Greenberg, Marilyn W. "A Study of the Reading Motivation of Twenty-Three Seventh-Grade Students." *Library Quarterly* (July 1970), 309-317.

Groff, Patrick J. "Textbooks Versus Tradebooks—A Child's View." *School Libraries* 16 (Summer 1967), 29-33.

Gruber, F. C. "Home Libraries of Junior High School Pupils." *English Journal* 21 (1932), 136-137.

Grumette, Jesse. "An Investigation into the Reading Tastes of First Year High School Students." *High Points* 16 (September 1934), 23-30.

Gunderson, Agnes G. "What Seven-Year-Olds Like in Books." *Journal of Educational Research* (March 1957), 509-520.

Gunzburg, Herbert C. "The Subnormal Boy and His Reading Interests." *Library Quarterly* 18 (October 1948), 264-274.

Hall, Lois B., and William N. Rairigh. "What Does Johnny Read?" *Maryland Libraries* 31 (Fall 1964), 6-8.

Hall, William E., and Francis Robinson. "The Role of Reading as a Life Activity in a Rural Community." *Journal of Applied Psychology* 26 (August 1942), 530-542.

Hardwick, Louise. "The Effect of a Personalized Reading Program on the Reading Skills, Attitudes, Study Habits, and Self-Concepts of Seventh Grade Students." Diss. University of California at Los Angeles, 1970.

Harris, Chester W. "Measurement of Comprehension of Literature and Its Relation to Enjoyment." Diss. University of Chicago, 1946.

Harris, James M. "The Expressed Reading Interest of First Grade Boys and Girls and the Adequacy of Current Basic Readers in Meeting These Interests." Diss. Cornell University, 1955.

Haskins, Jack B. "Title-Rating: A Method for Measuring Reading

Interests and Predicting Readership." *Educational and Psychological Measurement* 20 (1960), 551-565.

Havens, Ruth M., and Ruth Andrus. "Desirable Literature for Children of Kindergarten Age." *Pedagogical Seminary and Journal of Genetic Psychology* 36 (September 1920), 390-412.

Heller, Frieda M. "Free Reading in the Junior High School." *Educational Research Bulletin* 19 (April 1940), 217-222, 243-244.

Helmkamp, E. H. "Appraising Reading Interests and Attitudes in Grades 10–14." *Evaluation in Reading.* Supplementary Educational Monographs, no. 88. Edited by H. M. Robinson. Chicago, Illinois: University of Chicago Press, 1958.

Henderson, F. D. "The Voluntary Reading of 2083 Junior and Senior High Pupils." *Bulletin of National Association of Secondary School Principals* 11 (1927), 81-83.

Hermans, Mabel C. "Utilizing Adolescent Interests." *Los Angeles Educational Research Bulletin* 10 (May-June 1931), 2-29.

Hildreth, Gertrude. *Teaching Reading.* New York: Holt, Rinehart & Winston, Inc., 1958.

Himmelweit, Hilda, et al. *Television and the Child.* New York: Oxford University Press, 1958.

Hoar, Jere. "Book Reading in the Senior Years: The Habits and Preferences of Two Hundred Mississippians." *Journal of Educational Sociology* 34 (November 1960), 137-144.

Hockett, John A. "Variations in Reading in Different School Grades." *Twelfth Yearbook of the California Elementary School Principals' Association,* 12 (1940), pp. 95-100.

Holy, T. C. *Survey of the Schools of Euclid, Ohio.* Ohio State University Studies, Bureau of Educational Research Monographs, no. 22. Columbus, Ohio: Ohio State University, 1936.

Hoole, William S. "A Cross-Section Survey of the Reading Habits

and Library Usage of Birmingham-Southern College Students."
Peabody Journal of Education 15 (January 1938), 216-220.

Horst, J. M. "Will They Read: An Experiment." *English Journal*
42 (May 1953), 260-262.

Hosic, James F. "Empirical Study in School Reading." *Teachers
College Contributions to Education,* no. 114. New York:
Bureau of Publications, Teachers College, Columbia University,
1921.

Houkom, A. F. *The Reading Interests of Educated People.* Thesis.
University of Illinois, 1933.

Houle, C. O. "What Adults Think of the Great Books." *School Review* 54 (May 1946), 270-278.

Howes, V. M. "Children's Interest." *Education* 83 (1963), 491-496.

Huber, Miriam B. "Children's Interests in Poetry." *Teachers College Record* 28 (October 1926), 93-104.

_____. "Influence of Intelligence upon Children's Reading Interests." *Teachers College Contributions to Education,* no. 312.
Bureau of Publications, Teachers College, Columbia University,
1928.

Huber, Miriam B., Herbert B. Bruner, and Charles M. Curry.
Children's Interests in Poetry. Chicago, Illinois: Rand McNally
and Company, 1927.

Hughes, Frances M. "A Survey of Reading Interests of Pupils of
Madison, Wisconsin, High School." *Education* 45 (March 1924),
437-438.

Hughes, M., and P. Willis. "Personal Reading: A Study of a
Seventh Grade." *On Becoming a Reader,* Proceedings of the
Claremont Reading Conference, 29 (1965), 90-101.

Hull, Raymona E. "Reading Interests of Technical Institute Freshmen, 1950." *Junior College Journal* 21 (January 1951), 292-297.

Husén, T. *Adolescensen: Undersökningar Rörande Manlig Svensk Ungdom I Aldern 17-20 Ar.* Stockholm, Sweden, 1944.

Irving, Arthur P. "Home Reading of School Children." *Pedagogical Seminary* 7 (1900), 138-140.

Jefferis, A. W. "A Study of Reading Interests of Young People in Industry." *Elementary School Journal* 28 (1928), 587-602.

Jefferson, Benjamin F. "Some Relationships between Parents' and Children's Preferences in Juvenile Literature." Diss. University of California at Berkeley, 1956.

————. "Some Relationships between Parents' and Children's Preferences in Juvenile Literature." *Elementary School Journal* 58 (January 1958), 212-218.

Jenkinson, A. J. *What Do Boys and Girls Read?* London: Methuen, 1940.

Jennings, Joe. "Leisure Reading of Junior High Boys and Girls." *Peabody Journal of Education* 6 (May 1929), 333-347.

Jesson-Dibley, David, and Earl Roland. "What Do They Read?" *English* 13 (Summer 1960), 55-58.

Jewett, Arno. "What Does Research Tell about the Reading Interests of Junior High Pupils?" *Improving Reading in the Junior High School.* Edited by A. Jewett, pp. 26-33. Washington, D.C.: Office of Education, U.S. Government Printing Office, 1958.

Johns, Jerry L. "Expressed Reading Preferences of Intermediate-Grade Students in Urban Settings." Diss. Michigan State University, 1970.

Johnson, Byron L. "An Investigation of the Reading Interests and Habits of Adults at Various Ages, Educational, and Occupational Levels." *School Review* 40 (January 1932), 33-43.

————. "Children's Reading Interests as Related to Sex and Grade in School." *School Review* 40 (April 1932), 258-272.

Johnson, Charles E., and J. Harlan Shores. "Reading and Reference Interests of Junior High Students." *Illinois Education* 51 (1963), 374-376.

Johnson, C. T. M. "A Study of the Reading Interests of Seventh and Eighth Grade Pupils in the Arden-Carmichael Union School District of Sacramento County, California." *Reading Instruction in the Secondary School.* Edited by Henry A. Bamman, Ursula Hogan, and Charles E. Greene. New York: David McKay Company, 1961.

Johnson, J. C. "Relationships between Attitudes Reflected in Thematic Content and Recalled Comprehension." *The Reading Teacher* 22 (1968), 276-277.

Jones, Harold D. "The Extracurricular Reading Interests of Students in a State College." *School and Society* 72 (1950), 40-43.

Jones, Margaret H., and Edward C. Caterette. "Redundancy in Children's Free-Reading Choices." *Journal of Verbal Learning and Verbal Behavior* 2 (December 1963), 489-493.

Jones, W. Stephen. "Private Reading in the Fifth." *Times Educational Supplement* 17 (September 1965), 506.

Jordan, Arthur M. *Children's Interests in Reading.* New York: Bureau of Publications, Teachers College, Columbia University, 1921.

———. *Children's Interest in Reading.* rev. ed. Chapel Hill, North Carolina: University of North Carolina Press, 1926.

Jung, Raymond. "Leisure Activities and Preferences of Children at Different Socio-Economic Status and from Different Ethnic Groups." Diss. University of California at Berkeley, 1963.

Jungeblut, Ann, and John Coleman. "Reading Content That Interests Seventh, Eighth, and Ninth Grade Students." *Journal of Educational Research* 58 (May-June 1969), 393-401.

Kammann, Richard. "Verbal Complexity and Preferences in Poetry." *Journal of Verbal Learning and Verbal Behavior* 5 (1966), 536-540.

Kangley, Lucy. "Poetry Preferences in the Junior High Schools." *Teachers College Contributions to Education,* no. 758. New York: Bureau of Publications, Teachers College, Columbia University, 1938.

Karlin, Robert. "Library Book Borrowing Versus Library Book Reading." *Reading Teacher* 16 (November 1962), 77-81.

King, Cora E. "Favorite Poems for Children of Elementary Age." *Teachers College Record* 23 (May 1922), 255-273.

King, Ethel M. "Critical Appraisal of Research on Children's Reading Interests, Preferences, and Habits." *Canadian Education and Research Digest* 7 (December 1967), 312-326.

Kiser, George. "A Study of Selected Indicators of Children's Interest-in-Reading." Diss. University of Kentucky, 1968.

Klein, Howard A. "Interest and Comprehension in Sex-Typed Materials." Diss. Syracuse University, 1968.

Kopel, David. "The Nature of Interests." *Education* 83 (1963), 597-602.

Kramer, M. I. "The Reading Preferences of Elementary and High School Pupils." *Catholic Educational Review* 37 (1939), 310-325.

Kujoth, Jean S., ed. *Reading Interests of Children and Young Adults.* Metuchen, New Jersey: The Scarecrow Press, Inc., 1970.

Kyte, George C. "Children's Reactions to Fifty Selected Poems." *Elementary School Journal* 47 (February 1947), 331-339.

LaBrant, Lou L. "The Use of Communication Media." *The Guinea Pigs after Twenty Years.* Edited by Margaret Willis, pp. 127-164. Columbus, Ohio: Ohio State University, 1961.

LaBrant, Lou L., and F. M. Heller. "An Evaluation of Free Reading in Grades Seven to Twelve Inclusive." *Contributions to Education*, no. 4. Columbus, Ohio: Ohio State University Press, 1939.

Lancaster, Thomas J. "A Study of the Voluntary Reading of Pupils in Grade Four through Eight." *Elementary School Journal* 28 (March 1928), 525-537.

Larsson, L. *Ungdom Läser*. Stockholm, Sweden, 1947.

Lazar, May. "Reading Interests, Activities, and Opportunities of Bright, Average, and Dull Children." *Teachers College Contributions to Education*, no. 707. New York: Bureau of Publications, Teachers College, Columbia University.

Leafe, B. "A Survey of Reading Interests and Habits of High School Students in the Sacramento Area." *Reading Instruction in the Secondary School*. Edited by Henry A. Bamman, Ursula Hogan, and Charles E. Greene. New York: David McKay Company, 1961.

Lehman, Harvey C. "Reading Books Just for Fun." *School Review* 34 (May 1926), 357-364.

Lehtovaara, A., and P. Saarinen. *School-Age Reading Interests: A Methodological Approach*. Helsinki, Sweden, 1964.

Leijonhielm, Ch. *Ungdomens Läsvanor*. Stockholm, Sweden, 1954.

Lewerenz, A. S. "An Experiment in Evaluating Books Read and Enjoyed by School Children." *Los Angeles Educational Research Bulletin* 9 (September 1929), 10-14.

Lewis, B. A. "Comparison of Kindergarten Teachers' Perceptions of Children's Preferences in Books with the Children's Actual Preferences." Diss. North Texas State University, 1970.

Lingeman, Richard R. "Middletown Now." *Pop Culture in America*. Edited by David M. White, pp. 257-267. Chicago, Illinois: Quadrangle Books, Inc., 1970.

Link, H. C., and H. A. Hope. *People and Books: A Study of Read-*

ing and Book Buying Habits. New York: Book Manufacturers Institute, 1946.

Logan, Chester. "What Students and Faculty Read." *Change* 4 (May 1972), 10-11.

Low, F. B. "Reading of the Modern Girl." *Nineteenth Century* 59 (1906), 278-287.

Ludwig, Merritt C. "Hard Words and Human Interest: Their Effects on Readership." *Journalism Quarterly* 26 (1949), 167-171.

Lynch, M. D. "Books Children Like and Why." *Parents Magazine* 5 (1930), 22-23, 83-86.

McAulay, J. D. "Interests of Elementary School Children." *Social Education* 26 (April 1962), 199-201.

Mackintosh, Helen K. "Recent Data on Children's Interests in Poetry." *Elementary English* 8 (January 1931), 18-20.

————. "A Study of Children's Choices in Poetry." *Elementary English* 1 (May 1924), 85-89.

Malchow, Evangeline C. "Reading Interests of Junior High School Pupils." *School Review* 45 (March 1937), 175-185.

Martin, D. R. "Attitude of an Age Group to Poetry." *British Journal of Educational Psychology* 17 (1947), 51-52.

Mary Consuelo, Sister. "What Do First Graders Like to Read?" *Catholic School Journal* 67 (February 1967), 42-43.

Mary Edith, Sister, and Sister May Amatora. "The Age Factor in Children's Interests in Free Reading." *Education* 71 (May 1951), 567-571.

Mason, Marcella. "Watching Children's Growth in Outside Reading." *Elementary English* 16 (October 1939), 221-222, 239.

Mauck, Inez L., and Esther J. Swenson. "A Study of Children's Recreational Reading." *Elementary School Journal* 50 (1949), 144-150.

May, M. A., and Melle L. Jenkinson. "Developing Interest in Reading with Film." *Audio-Visual Communication Review* 1 (1953), 159-166.

Maz, V. "Radio Listening, Televiewing, and Reading Habits of Pittsburgh Public High School Students." *Pittsburgh Schools* 27 (1953), 156-172.

McCarty, Pearl S. "Reading Interest Shown by Choices of Books in School Libraries." *School Review* 58 (1950), 90-96.

McCloskey, Elinor F. "A Study of the Free Reading Habits of Sixth Grade Negro Boys Living in Disadvantaged Areas in the City of New York." Diss. Columbia University, 1966.

McCullough, Constance. "What Is a Good Book to a Ninth Grader?" *English Journal* 25 (May 1936), 381-387.

McElroy, Elizabeth W. "Subject Variety in Adult Reading: Factors Related to Variety in Reading." *Library Quarterly* 38 (1968), 154-167.

McEwin, Charles K. "The Relationship of Selected Factors Associated with Middle Class Oriented Reading Materials to the Preferences of Socio-Economic Groups for Pictorial Representations and Story Themes." Diss. North Texas State University, 1971.

McKay, James. "A Summary of Scientific Research and Professional Literature on Reading Interests." Diss. University of Pittsburgh, 1968.

McReynolds, Janet K. "A Study of Common Aspects Found in Selected Literature for Adolescents—1966 to 1970." Diss. Southern Illinois University, 1971.

Meckel, Henry C. "An Exploratory Study of the Responses of Adolescent Pupils to Situations in a Novel." Diss. University of Chicago, 1946.

Melbro, Irving R. "A Review of the Literature on Children's Interests." *Twelfth Yearbook of the California Elementary School Principals' Association* 12 (1940), 95-100.

Mendenhall, James E. and Marcie E. "The Influence of Familiarity upon Children's Preferences for Pictures and Poems." Diss. Columbia University, 1933.

Milam, Carl H. *Children's Reading: A Study of the Voluntary Reading of Boys and Girls in the United States.* Report of the Subcommittee on Reading, White House Conference on Child Health and Protection. New York: Century, 1932.

Miller, Arthur L. "A Study of Reading Tastes of Children in Grades Four, Five, and Six in Selected Schools of the Lamar Area School Study Council." Diss. University of Houston, 1966.

Miner, Lilian B. "Voluntary Reading in the English High School." *School Review* 12 (1905), 180-188.

Monson, Dianne L. "Children's Test Responses to Seven Humorous Stories." *Elementary School Journal* 68 (1968), 334-339.

Monto, Saima W. "An Analysis of the Reading Interests of Junior and Senior High School Pupils." *Bulletin of the National Association of Secondary School Principals* 24 (January 1929), 96-98.

Moreland, G. B. "What Young People Want to Read About." *Library Quarterly* 10 (1940), 469-493.

Mott, John H. "Reading Interests of Adolescents: A Critical Study of Fifty Years of Research." Diss. University of Northern Colorado, 1970.

Munson, Gorham. "Who Are Our Favorite Nineteenth Century Authors?" *English Journal* 33 (March 1944), 113-118.

National Opinion Research Center. *What, Where, Why, Do People Read?* Denver, Colorado, 1946.

Nelms, Ben F. "Characteristics of Poetry Associated with Preferences of a Panel of Tenth Grade Students." Diss. University of Iowa, 1967.

Nelson, Richard C. "Children's Poetry Preferences." *Elementary English* 43 (1966), 247-251.

Norvell, George W. "Some Results of a Twelve-Year Study of Children's Reading Interests." *English Journal* 35 (December 1946), 531-536.

———. *The Reading Interests of Young People*. Boston, Massachusetts: D. C. Heath and Company, 1950.

———. *What Boys and Girls Like to Read*. Morristown, New Jersey: Silver Burdett Company, 1958.

Novotny, Lorene. "A Study of the Reading Interests of Slow-Learning Children in the Seventh Grade." Thesis. University of Kansas, 1954.

Ojala, William T., and Marda McNeill. "A Survey of Adolescent Interests in Three Schools." *Arizona English Bulletin* 14 (April 1972), pp. 96-108.

Olson, Arthur V., and Carl L. Rosen. "A Comparison of Reading Interests of Two Populations of Ninth Grade Students." *Adolescence* 1 (Winter 1966-1967), 321-326.

Packer, Athol B. "A Study of Factors Involved in the Selection of Free Reading Materials by Fourth Graders." Diss. University of Kansas, 1967.

Parker, Beryl, and Franc J. Thyny. "Tastes Differ." *Educational Method* 19 (December 1939), 162-167.

Parsons, Rhey B. "A Study of Adult Reading." Thesis. University of Illinois, 1923.

Payne, I. M. "Poetry Preferences in the Fourth Year of the Secondary School." *Education Review* 16 (1963), 63-70.

Peel, E. A. "The Analysis of Preferences." *Research Design and the Teaching of English*. Edited by David H. Russell et al. Urbana, Illinois: National Council of Teachers of English, 1964.

Peller, Lili. "Reading and Daydreams in Latency, Boy-Girl Differences." *Journal of the American Psychoanalytic Association* 6 (1958), 57-70.

———. "Daydreams and Children's Favorite Books: Psychoanalytic Comments." *The Psychoanalytic Study of the Child* 14 (1959), 414-433.

Peltola, Bette J. "A Study of Children's Book Choices." *Elementary English* 40 (November 1963), 690-695, 707.

———. "A Study of the Indicated Literary Choices and Measured Literary Knowledge of Fourth and Sixth Grade Boys and Girls." Diss. University of Minnesota, 1965.

Persing, C. L., and H. R. Sattley. "Discovering Reading Interests of Maladjusted Students." *Bulletin of American Library Association* 29 (January 1935), 13-23.

Peterson, Anna. "Leisure Reading of High School Pupils." *Education* 54 (1934), 296-300.

Pittman, Grace. "Young Children Enjoy Poetry." *Elementary English* 43 (1966), 56-59.

Porcella, Brewster. "A Summary of Research on the Reading Interests and Habits of College Graduates." *Occasional Papers*, no. 74. Urbana, Illinois: University of Illinois Graduate School of Library Science, 1964.

Postman, Neil. *Television and the Teaching of English*. Urbana, Illinois: National Council of Teachers of English, 1961.

Powell, A. S. "Reading Interests of 366 College Students." *Journal of Negro Education* 23 (1954), 183-185.

Powell, Florence. "Students' Choice." *Library Journal* 76 (March 15, 1951), 488-490.

Prescott, Katherine. "A Study of the Interests of Adult Readers, Norwood Branch, Cleveland Public Library." Thesis. Western Reserve University, 1954.

Price, Ron and Christine. "What Do Freshmen and Sophomores Like to Read?" *Arizona English Bulletin* (April 1970), 13-19.

Punke, H. H. "The Home and Adolescent Reading Interests." *School Review* 45 (1937), 612-620.

Rankin, Earl F., and Charlotte L. Thames. "A Methodology for Studying Children's Reactions to Stories in First Grade Readers." *The Reading Teacher* 22 (1968), 242-245.

Rankin, Marie. "Children's Interests in Library Books of Fiction." *Teachers College Contributions to Education,* no. 906. New York: Bureau of Publications, Teachers College, Columbia University, 1944.

Raymond, Ruth. "Free Reading in World Literature." *English Journal* 49 (March 1955), 160-162.

Reed, Charles H. "Relationships of Personality and Reading Choices of Sixth Grade Children." Diss. University of California at Berkeley, 1962.

Reinhardt, Emma. "Reading Interests of Freshmen in a Teachers College." *Teachers College Journal* 2 (November 1930), 57-60, 63.

Rice, Richard, and James Sellers. "What Do Teenagers Read?" *International Journal of Religious Education* 37 (October 1960), 6-7, 38.

Ridgway, R. W. "A Study of the Readability, Interest, and Usefulness of Selected Materials for Retarded Readers in Grades Four to Eight." *Kansas University Bulletin of Education* 10 (1955), 10-14.

Rinehart, Anne C. "What Pittsburgh High School Students Read." *School Betterment Studies* 2, no. 1 (1930), 9-83.

_____. "What Pittsburgh Junior High School Pupils Read." *School Betterment Studies* 3, no. 1 (1931), 84.

Roberts, C. R., and R. A. Davis. "Reading Interests of Teachers."

Educational Administration and Supervision 15 (February 1929), 102-116.

Robinson, H. M. "What Research Says to the Teacher of Reading— Reading Interests." *The Reading Teacher* 8 (1955), 173-177, 191.

Roderick, Jessie A. "Some Relationships between Creativity and the Reading Preferences and Choices of a Group of Sixth Graders." Diss. Temple University, 1967.

Rogers, Helen E., and H. Alan Robinson. "Reading Interests of First Graders." *Elementary English* 40 (November 1963), 707-711.

Root, R. W., and P. M. Schrock. "Reader Interest Research with Children." *Journalism Quarterly* 41 (1964), 443-444.

Rosenblatt, Louise M. "Development of Reading Interests and Critical Appreciation in Secondary Schools and Colleges." *Reading and Pupil Development*. Edited by William S. Gray, pp. 223-229. Chicago, Illinois: University of Chicago Press, 1940.

Rothney, John, and Robert McCaul. "Reading Preferences of High School Boys." *English Journal* 27 (October 1938), 650-660.

Row, Barbara H. "Reading Interests of Elementary School Pupils in Selected Schools in Muscogee County, Georgia." Diss. Auburn University, 1968.

Rowland, Monroe, and Patricia R. Hill. "Race, Illustrations, and Interest in Materials for Reading and Creative Writing." *Journal of Negro Education* 34 (Winter 1965), 84-87.

Royster, Sallibelle. "Reading Tastes of Twelfth Grade Pupils." *Education* 56 (February 1936), 369-371.

————. "What High School Freshmen Like to Read." *English Journal* 22 (1933), 137-139.

Rudman, Herbert C. "The Informational Needs and Reading Interests of Children in Grades 4–8." *Elementary School Journal* 55 (1955), 502-512.

Russell, David H. "Reading Preferences of Younger Adolescents in Saskatchewan." *English Journal* 30 (1941), 131-136.

Rydor, Sarah. "What Ethnic Solidarity." *Integrated Education* 7 (November 1969), 39-42.

Saine, Lynette. "Relationships of Selected Factors to Reading Interests of Negro College Students." Diss. University of Chicago, 1950.

Sakamoto, I. Hayashi, and M. Kamei. "A Developmental Study on the Points of Inspiration in Reading." *The Science of Reading* 10 (1967), 1-9.

Sauls, Charles W. "The Relationship of Selected Factors to the Recreational Reading of Sixth Grade Students." Diss. Louisiana State University, 1971.

Scanlon, William J. "One Hundred Most Popular Books of Children's Fiction Selected by Children." *Elementary English* 25 (February 1948), 83-97.

Schmidt, Sheldon L. "A Study of the Development of Self-Commitment to Independent Reading in Uncommitted Fourth Grade Students." Diss. University of North Dakota, 1970.

Schramm, William L. "Why Adults Read." *National Social Studies Education Yearbook* (1955), 57-58.

Scott, Walter J. *Reading, Film and Radio Tastes of High School Boys and Girls.* Educational Research Series, no. 28. Wellington, New Zealand: Council for Educational Research, 1947.

Seegers, J. C. "A Study of Children's Reading." *Elementary English* 13 (November 1936), 251-254.

Shatter, Aubrey. "A Survey of Student Reading." *English Journal* 40 (May 1951), 271-273.

Shnayer, Sidney W. "Some Relationships between Reading Interest and Reading Comprehension." Diss. University of California at Berkeley, 1967.

————. "Some Relationships between Reading Interest and Reading Comprehension." *Reading and Realism,* Proceedings of the Thirteenth Annual Convention. Newark, Delaware: International Reading Association, 1969.

Shores, J. Harlan. "Reading Interests and Informational Needs of Children in Grades Four to Eight." *Elementary English* 31 (December 1954), 493-500.

————. "Reading Interests and Informational Needs of High School Students." *Reading Teacher* (April 1964), 536-544.

Simpson, Ray H., and Anthony T. Soares. "Best and Least Liked Short Stories in Junior High School." *English Journal* 54 (February 1965), 108-111.

Sizemore, Robert A. "Reading Interests in Junior High School." *Education* 83 (1963), 473-479.

————. "The Reading Interests and Preferences of Deviates in Mental Ability and Educational Attainment in the Seventh and Eighth Grades." Diss. Northwestern University, 1961.

Sletvold, S. *Barna og Litteraturen.* Oslo, Norway, 1958.

Smiley, J. "Children's Interests and a Free-Reading Program." *English Journal* 41 (1952), 479-484.

Smith, Dora V. "Current Issues Relating to Development of Reading Interests and Tastes." *Recent Trends in Reading.* Supplementary Educational Monographs, no. 49. Edited by W. S. Gray, pp. 297-306. Chicago, Illinois: University of Chicago Press, 1939.

————. *Evaluating Instruction in Secondary School English: A Report of a Division of the New York Regents' Inquiry into the Character and Cost of Public Education in New York.* Urbana, Illinois: National Council of Teachers of English, 1941.

Smith, Franklin O. "Pupils' Voluntary Reading." *Pedagogical Seminary* 14 (June 1907), 208-222.

Smith, George D. "The Nature of Student Reading." Diss. University of Chicago, 1946.

Smith, H. K. "A Survey of Current Reading in Grades Ten through Fourteen." *Developing Permanent Interests in Reading.* Supplementary Educational Monographs, no. 84. Edited by H. M. Robinson, pp. 65-68. Chicago, Illinois: University of Chicago Press, 1956.

Smith, Mary L., and Isabel V. Eno. "What Do They Really Want to Read?" *English Journal* 50 (May 1961), 343-345.

Smith, Nila B. "An Investigation in Children's Interests in Different Types of Stories." *Detroit Educational Bulletin* 9 (February 1926), 3-4.

Smith, Ruth C. "Children's Reading Choices and Basic Reader Content." *Elementary English* 39 (March 1962), 202-209.

Soares, Anthony T. "Interest and Content in Some Recreational Reading of Junior High School Students." Diss. University of Idaho, 1962.

_____. "Salient Elements of Recreational Reading of Junior High School Students." *Elementary English* 40 (December 1963), 843-845.

Soares, Anthony T., and Ray H. Simpson. "Interest in Recreational Reading of Junior High School Students." *Journal of Reading* 11 (October 1967), 14-21.

Stanchfield, Jo Martha C. "A Study of Boys' Reading Interests in Relationship to Reading Achievement." Diss. University of California, 1960.

_____. "Boys' Reading Interests as Revealed through Personal Conferences." *Reading Teacher* 16 (September 1962), 41-44.

_____. "The Reading Interests of Eighth Grade Boys." *Journal of Developmental Reading* (Summer 1962), 256-265.

Sterner, Alice P. "Radio, Motion Picture, and Reading Interests: A Study of High School Pupils." *Teachers College Contributions to Education*, no. 932. New York: Bureau of Publications, Teachers College, Columbia University, 1947.

Stevenson, Margaret T. "The Reading Interests of Grade Five Pupils." Diss. University of Alberta at Edmonton, 1969.

Stone, John P. "Factors Influencing Reading Choices." Thesis. University of Illinois, 1930.

Strang, Ruth. *Exploration in Reading Patterns*. Chicago, Illinois: University of Chicago Press, 1942.

————. "Reading Interests." *English Journal* 35 (November 1946), 477-482.

————. "The Scope of Adolescent Interests." *Education* 83 (1963), 463-467.

Stroh, Mary M. "Literature for Grades VII, VIII, and IX." *Teachers College Contributions to Education*, no. 232. New York: Bureau of Publications, Teachers College, Columbia University, 1926.

Taylor, Marion W., and Mary Schneider. "What Books Are Our Children Reading? The Reading Interests of Upper-Grade Pupils." *Chicago School Journal* 38 (January-February 1957), 155-160.

"Teen Reading Assessed in Scholastic's Survey." *Publishers' Weekly* 175 (April 13, 1959), 22-23.

Terman, Lewis, and Margaret Lima. *Children's Reading: A Guide for Parents and Teachers*. 2nd ed. New York: D. Appleton and Company, 1931.

Thompson, Evelyn S. "A Study of Voluntary Reading of Children in Grades Four, Five, and Six in Houston, Texas." Diss. Colorado State College, 1956.

Thorndike, Edward L. "Note on the Shifts of Interest with Age." *Journal of Applied Psychology* 33 (February 1949), 55-58.

Thorndike, Robert L., and Florence Henry. "Differences in Reading Interests Related to Differences in Sex and Intelligence Level." *Elementary School Journal* 40 (1940), 251-263.

Thurber, C. H. "Voluntary Reading of the Classical High School." *School Review* 13 (1905), 171.

True, M. B. C. "What My Children Read." *Education* 10 (1889), 42-45.

Vandament, William E., and W. A. Thalman. "An Investigation into the Reading Interests of Children." *Journal of Educational Research* 49 (1956), 467-470.

Vaughn, Beryl. "Reading Interests of Eighth Grade Students." *Journal of Developmental Reading* 6 (Spring 1963), 149-155.

Vinton, Iris. "What the City Boy Reads." *Elementary English* 40 (1963), 559-562.

Vostrovsky, C. "Children's Tastes in Reading." *Pedagogical Seminary* 6 (1899), 523-538.

Wade, Elizabeth. "Expressed Reading Preferences of Second Grade Children in Selected Schools in Colorado." *Childhood Education* 40 (May 1964), 494-495.

Wagner, Martha. "College Students Evaluate High School Reading." *English Journal* 41 (May 1952), 251-253.

Walberg, H. J. "Reading and Study Habits of High School Physics Students." *Journal of Reading* 11 (1968), 327-332, 383-389.

Waples, Douglas. "Reading Interests of Teachers." *United States Office of Education's National Survey of the Education of Teachers*, pp. 247-284. Washington, D.C.: U. S. Government Printing Office, 1935.

_____. "The Relation of Subject Interests to Actual Reading." *Library Quarterly* 2 (January 1932), 42-70.

Waples, Douglas, and Ralph Tyler. *What People Want to Read About*. Chicago, Illinois: American Library Association and The University of Chicago Press, 1931.

Washburne, Carleton W., and Mabel Vogel. *What Children Like to Read: The Winnetka Graded Book List*. Chicago, Illinois: American Library Association, 1926.

Webb, Marion A. "Children's Reading Tastes: A City Survey of Present Trends." *Publishers' Weekly* (March 26, 1932), 1469-1471.

Weekes, Blanche. "The Influence of Meaning on Children's Choices of Poetry." *Teachers College Contributions to Education*, no. 354. New York: Bureau of Publications, Teachers College, Columbia University, 1929.

Weingarten, Samuel. "Developmental Values in Voluntary Reading." *School Review* 42 (April 1954), 222-230.

_____. "Student Veterans' Reading Preferences." *Journal of Higher Education* 20 (June 1949), 299-302+.

Weiser, A. B., and E. J. Ashbaugh. "What Books Do Junior and Senior High School Students Read?" *Educational Research Bulletin* 3 (1924), 223-228, 250-253, 265-266.

Wells, Ruth E. "A Study of Tastes in Humorous Literature among Pupils of Junior and Senior High Schools." *Journal of Educational Research* 28 (October 1934), 81-91.

West, Guy A., and Floyd F. Caldwell. "Student and Teacher Preference in Literature." *California Quarterly of Secondary Education* 9 (October 1933), 19-22.

Wetzner, J., and R. L. Lyman. "The Development of Reading Interests and Tastes." *The Teaching of Reading: A Second Report*. Thirty-Sixth Yearbook of the National Society for the Study of Education, Part I, pp. 185-205. Bloomington, Illinois: Public Schools' Publishing Company, 1937.

Wheeler, Theodora. "Reading in the Lives of Young Girls." *Journal of Educational Psychology* 11 (December 1920), 481-501.

White, G. E. "Surveying Reading in a High School Community." *English Journal* 31 (1942), 669-672.

Whitehead, Frank. "The Attitudes of Grammar School Pupils towards Some Novels Commonly Read in Schools." *British Journal of Educational Psychology* 26 (1956), 104-111.

Whitman, Robert S. "Significant Reading Experiences of Superior English Students." *Illinois English Bulletin* 51 (February 1964), 1-14.

Wickens, A. R. "A Survey of Current Reading Interests in Grades 7-9." *Developing a Permanent Interest in Reading.* Supplementary Educational Monographs, no. 84. Edited by H. M. Robinson, pp. 60-64. Chicago, Illinois: University of Chicago Press, 1956.

Wiggins, Rudolph V. "A Comparison of Children's Interest in and Attitude towards Reading Material Written in Standard and Black English Forms." Diss. Ohio State University, 1971.

Willett, G. W. "The Reading Interests of High School Pupils." *English Journal* 8 (1919), 474-487.

Wissler, C. "Interests of Children in Reading in the Elementary School." *Pedagogical Seminary* 5 (1899), 523-546.

Wittick, Mildred L. "Sequential Development in Reading Interests and Tastes." *Sequential Development of Reading Abilities.* Supplementary Educational Monographs, no. 90, pp. 150-156. Chicago, Illinois: University of Chicago Press, 1960.

Witty, Paul. "A Study of Pupils' Interests: Grades Nine, Ten, Eleven, Twelve." *Education* 82 (October 1961), 100-110.

_____. "Current Role and Effectiveness of Reading among Youth." *Reading in High School and College.* Forty-Seventh Yearbook, Part II, National Society for the Study of Education.

Edited by Nelson B. Henry, pp. 8-26. Chicago, Illinois: University of Chicago Press, 1948.

————. "Some Interests of High School Boys." *Improvement of Reading through Classroom Practice*, IRA Conference Proceedings, vol. 9. Edited by J. A. Figurel, pp. 186-198. Newark, Delaware: International Reading Association, 1964.

Witty, Paul, et al. "Studies of Children's Interests: A Brief Summary, Part II." *Elementary English* 37 (1960), 540-545.

Witty, Paul, and Ann Coomer. "Activities and Preferences of a Secondary School Group." *Journal of Educational Psychology* 24 (February 1943), 65-76.

Witty, Paul, Ann Coomer, and D. McBean. "Children's Choices of Favorite Books: A Study Conducted in Ten Elementary Schools." *Journal of Educational Psychology* 37 (1946), 266-278.

Witty, Paul, and David Kopel. *Reading and the Educative Process*. Boston, Massachusetts: Ginn and Company, 1939.

Witty, Paul, and Harvey C. Lehman. "The Reading and Reading Interests of Gifted Children." *Journal of Genetic Psychology* 45 (September 1934), 466-548.

Wollner, M. H. B. "Children's Voluntary Reading as an Expression of Individuality." *Teachers College Contributions to Education*, no. 944. New York: Bureau of Publications, Teachers College, Columbia University, 1949.

Woolcock, Cyril. "The Reading of Superior Students in a Special High School." *Reading Teacher* 16 (May 1963), 448-451.

Worley, S. E. "Developmental Task Situations in Stories." *Reading Teacher* 21 (1967), 145-148.

Zais, Robert S. "A Scale to Measure Sophistication of Reading Interests." *Journal of Reading* 12 (1969), 273-276.

————. "The Sophistication of Reading Interests as Related to

Selected Personality Factors and Certain Other Characteristics of High School Students." Diss. University of Connecticut, 1968.

Zamchick, David. "Paperback Buying Patterns." *English Journal* 49 (1960), 336-340.

Zeligs, Rose. "Children's Opinions of Newbery Prize Books." *Elementary English Review* 17 (October 1940), 218.

_____. "What Sixth Grade Children Are Reading." *Elementary English Review* 14 (November 1937), 257-262.

Zeller, Dale. "The Relative Importance of Factors of Interest in Reading Materials of Junior High School Pupils." *Teachers College Contributions to Education,* no. 841. New York: Bureau of Publications, Teachers College, Columbia University, 1941.

Zimet, Sara. "Children's Interests and Story Preferences." *Elementary School Journal* 67 (1966), 122-130.

Studies of the Teaching of Literature

Although from the dire statements of directors of educational research about the overabundance of treatment studies one would expect a superfluity in research dealing with the teaching of literature, such is not the case. Of the few "experimental" studies that have been done, nearly all seem to fall into seven semi-discrete categories:

Studies in which the treatment variable is the material
Studies in which the treatment variable is the instructional technique
Evaluations of curricula
Studies of extensive reading
Studies of individualized reading programs
Studies in which literature is the treatment variable for some instructional end like writing or reading
Studies dealing with teachers and teacher training

A. Changes in Material

There are relatively few studies in this area. Most of them are experimental, although one does seek to relate the knowledge of students to the material they are required to read (Roberts, 1967). The researcher found that the meanings of approximately one half of the allusions presented in ninth grade literature anthologies could be identified by ninth grade students. Such a study might be interpreted in two ways: that the selections are too difficult or that it is more important to teach allusions or to write footnotes than one had imagined.

Although the Roberts study comments on the material that exists, the others seek to provide new material. In general these studies demonstrate the efficacy of relevant selections in instruction. A number of variations have been tried: modern literature for young adults in 1928 (Bernard, Anderson, and Raburn); advanced literature for gifted children in 1929 (Danielson); thematically relevant material in college courses in 1959 (Boehner); junior novels for adolescents in 1963 (Blount); materials geared to special socioeconomic groups in 1964 (Hogue); song lyrics in 1968 (Glenn); and "short, fast-moving fiction" in 1969 (Telford). Each variation was relevant to its audience in a slightly different way and each variation enjoyed some success. Most of the measures of success were questionnaires about the students' liking of the materials or the course, and those measures tended to confirm the hopes of the experimenter. Two of the studies did not find an effect: Glenn found that using song lyrics and related literature did not affect "sensitivity to literature," and Hogue found that the use of socioeconomically directed materials did not affect reading achievement or self-perception, although it did affect the attitudes toward reading of the third grade children.

Blount's (1963) study went farther than the others in that the researcher was concerned with the effect of the material in bringing students into congruence with expert judgment about the ideal novel. Using a Q-sort, Blount found the junior novel to be as effective as the adult novel in bringing students' concepts into agreement with those of the experts. Blount's study raised questions about treatment studies in general, but it did corroborate the critical principle of Frye and others that any novel—be it the junior novel or the adult novel (or perhaps even the children's novel)—has persistent characteristics and can be used to teach students about the larger type. In another study, Brownell, Meredith, and Nicol (1967) found that there was no significant difference whether outside literature or the students' own writing was used as examples of literary devices or to stimulate critical responses in fourth, fifth, and sixth grades. Students liked all of the courses.

Obviously the research in this area is skimpy and more could be done, particularly research with the use of ethnic material, but one wonders what form the research might take. Blount has indicated that any work can be used to teach a literary concept. His study might be verified with ethnic literature or comic strips or films. The other studies have hinted that changing material order will not substantially affect the learning of students, much as they might like to read literature that seems closer to them. If experimental research manipulating literary content is undertaken, teaching method must also be manipulated or at least controlled. Further, the criterion must be something other than the liking of the material or the lesson itself. A literature lesson is both a valid experience in its own right and instrumental to some skill, attitude, or understanding. Experimental research must look at the instrumentality of the lesson as well as at its essence.

B. Changes in Instructional Method

Under this heading, the first question to be addressed is whether the explicit teaching of literature has any effects at all, and, if so, what these effects are. A pioneer study in this area was that of Broening (1929), who found that fourth and fifth grade children who were given literature lessons including role playing, writing, field trips, reading, and pantomime gained significantly in number and range of books read freely, in ranking of reading as a pursuit, and in a test of literary discrimination which asked them to pick the original version of a text from a group of selections which included two or three perversions. Earlier Ruhlen (1926) had found that if students were taught a difficult poem, they would do better on a test about that poem's imagery and allusions. Much more recently, a study showed that when college freshmen were taught novels, their response patterns to the novels changed (Wilson, 1963). The patterns were measured using Squire's categories, and the students showed a mean gain of 23.9 percent in the use of interpretational responses (in the other categories there was a decrease). In a similar study Sanders (1970) found that teaching interpretation based on guided activities and on a discussion of the responses of ninth graders produced significant (.01) differences in quality, amount, and pattern of response, as well as in fluency of response. A group taught to interpret shifted its responses from the literary judgment to the interpretational comment. Text differences were nonsignificant. Another study (Compere, 1952) found that students in college tended to dislike poetry, and their dislike was correlated with the teacher's use of a prescribed text, recitation technique, biographical emphasis, metrical emphasis, and required memorization. All of these studies indicate that instruction affects taste and style of response, but, as Broening notes, the studies do not indicate what background factors and what treatment factors most influenced the gain.

A small group of studies have looked at manipulation of content or focus of attention as the prime experimental variable. One found that attention to rhythm and metaphor did not affect the discriminatory abilities of college students (Leopold, 1933). Another found that such teaching did affect the ability to make inferences, discriminate arguments, and recognize assumptions (Koob, 1946). In a third study the experimenter focused the students' attention on the profundity of themes with only slight gain on an understanding test and a test asking the students to determine profundity (Anderson, 1969). A fourth study found that teaching general semantics had no effect on college students' responses to a poem judged on whether they read the poem literally or symbolically (Livingston, 1969). None of these studies controls well for teaching as a variable, and the whole notion of such studies is methodologically suspect. One study which showed the faults in the method was that of Smith (1968), who tried to see if changing the writing assignment would improve the students' attitudes toward what they read. Trying a creative and a close-ended writing assignment given before the reading of a story but to be done after the reading, Smith found that the close-ended assignment produced significantly more favorable attitudes toward the story. It is possible to interpret this finding in two ways. Certainly one way is to consider that the most important variables, teaching strategy and teacher personality, have been neglected. Another way is to consider that the assignment made sense and helped the story make sense. We cannot tell which interpretation to make.

When we come to studies dealing with teaching strategy, we find they fall into two rough groups: those which deal with modes of presentation and those which deal with teacher behavior. In the first group, Prettyman (1965) found that teaching Victorian literature by the lecture method produced better results than the activity method on teacher-made tests covering recall of the material. Another study found no difference among three groups of college students taught modern literature by television, lecture, or discussion (Becker et al., 1957). Two of the more thorough studies in this area dealt with oral presentation of the text and with film. The first treated of students who were given poem texts without oral presentation, poem texts with presentation, presentation alone, and preparation of discussion of a similar poem, and a multiple-choice test on the sense, structure, technique, and meaning of the poems read (Knapp, 1960). The students who discussed the texts did better than the silent readers; the listeners and readers did better than either the listeners or the readers. As the experiment went on, the differences decreased between the mean scores of groups on segments of the test. Knapp inferred that the test itself taught as much as any of the experimental variables. The first finding of the study was partly confirmed by Vergara (1946), who found that on the Hartley tests of poetry college-age listeners did significantly better than readers.

Vergara's study is one of the more elaborate in the field, building as it does from case study to semi-controlled sample to highly controlled sample. She devised a measure of understanding sense and mood, using the free responses of students as the criteria for best answers. On this measure there were no significant differences. Her case studies touch upon college students' lack of interest in poetry, and her conclusion is that barriers to liking poetry include personal factors, such as intellect, experience, and prejudice, and prior teaching, which had turned them into frustrated symbol hunters.

The other study dealt with the use of a filmed version of a story before and after the reading of the story. The criterion was a test of understanding; the subjects were junior high school students. Film viewing improved achievement, and film viewing before the reading did so only slightly more than film viewing after the reading. There were individual differences among films, some being effective with all groups, others effective only with groups having higher IQ's (Levinson, 1962). This study was partially confirmed by Hoetker's (1971) study of theatre going and its relation to the understanding of and liking of plays; timing of attendance seemed to play no significant role in the understanding or attitudes of students. Hoetker's is possibly the best worked out of all experimental studies in the field.

The studies of teaching method in fine rather than in gross have examined such matters as inductive and deductive teaching (La-Rocque, 1965); inductive and programmed teaching (Weiss, 1968); teaching emphasizing divergent and that emphasizing convergent thinking (Hackett, Brown, and Michael, 1968); and structured and nonstructured teaching (Grindstaff, 1968; Monson, 1968; Morris, 1970). Using elaborately designed and controlled lessons, LaRocque found that deductive methods of teaching figurative language to eighth grade students produced better results on an achievement test than did inductive methods. Weiss, on the other hand, found that inductive teaching of poetry produced more statements in the categories of perception and evaluation (using the Purves and Rippere categories) from eleventh grade students. On a subsequent test, these gains persisted—there were no changes in the use of engagement or evaluation. If one thinks of such gains as improvement (that is, a movement toward the habits of professional critics), then inductive teaching seems to promote that kind of learning; it does not promote the learning of specific content, such as the identification of figurative language.

Hackett, Brown, and Michael (1968) investigated the minimal use of threats to self-esteem, student participation in the development of creative learning, and divergent thinking as the experimental variables. The students, twelfth graders, read *Antigone* and then took a multiple-choice and an essay test. The results indicate the success of the experimental groups (there was some teacher effect apparent on one measure). Morris's sixth graders did no better or worse on a test of understanding, whether the lessons were structured or unstructured. Grindstaff conducted a somewhat similar study with tenth grade students, but the experimental variables were structural analysis or "new criticism" and experimental reflective analyses based on the readers' initial responses. Her criterion consisted of essays on each of four novels—one written before and one after instruction, each essay analyzed using Squire's categories. Significant differences (.05) occurred in four categories (narrational, associational, interpretational, and literary judgment). The reflective group was more divergent than the new critical group; a control group had more reading difficulties than did either experimental group. Grindstaff's study supported those of Hackett, Brown, and Michael and of Weiss, as well as those of Wilson and Sanders. If the criteria are divergent thinking and personal response, the less directive the instruction the better. If the goal is convergence, as in LaRocque's study or in Monson's, where the end was finding the humorous aspect of humorous works, more highly structured and teacher-centered teaching will be effective. Monson's study (looking at fifth grade students) was the only one of this group that dealt specifically with students from low socioeconomic groups, and she found structured teaching most fruitful with those groups. When left to find the humor themselves, they had trouble. In this study the measure was also the teaching instrument, much as had been the case with Knapp's study.

These studies confirmed the obvious inference from all of the treatment studies: depending on the criterion, the same treatments will be more or less successful. If one is looking for specific answers, directive teaching toward those answers will be successful; if one is looking for divergence, nondirective teaching will be successful. We have seen that the Squire or the Purves and Rippere categories have been used as criteria for several studies. At times the investigator has wanted a certain category of response to emerge, at times, a diversity of categories. Either goal is appropriate, depending upon other circumstances. Effective method seems to vary with goal. For the curriculum maker, then, there seems to be a more organic relationship between goal and method than many polemecists of education would have it.

C. Curriculum Evaluations

So far in this chapter we have been dealing with evaluation of content and method. Now we turn briefly to evaluation of curricular arrangements, the architecture of instruction. We turn briefly because curricular evaluation is or should be tied to the curriculum in question, so that its evaluation often has only a nonce value.

In a sense a review of curriculum evaluation must begin with the Eight-Year Study undertaken to evaluate the effectiveness of progressive education (Smith and Tyler, 1942). We have discussed some of the measures created in chapter 1, but, to summarize, there were three appreciation questionnaires: the novel questionnaire, the drama questionnaire, and the questionnaire on voluntary reading. These measures of the students' attitudes and interests were the backbone of the literature part of the study; they were subjected to validity studies and came through fairly well. Cognitive tests on interpretation, critical-mindedness, and judging the effectiveness of writing were also developed but not so fully field tested. In addition, there were book reading records in which works read could be classified by type and maturity level, and there were magazine, newspaper, radio, and motion picture checklists. To a great extent, this study has served as a model for summative evaluation of a curriculum and should continue to do so. One follow-up study found that reading habits persisted for twenty years after schooling (Willis, 1961).

The only comparable study is that done by Dressel and Mayhew (1954) to evaluate general education and, for our purposes, humanities courses. They developed a humanities attitude inventory, a humanities vocabulary test, a "Guide to Critical Analysis and Judgment in the Humanities," and a humanities participation inventory, with subscores for frequency, enjoyment, and serious-ness. In addition, there were general measures of critical thinking and attitudes. The results of the study are quite dismal—humani-ties courses failed in their objectives by a few measures that were tried—but the breadth of the measures, like that of the measures developed for the Eight-Year Study, are worthy of emulation. An-other model for curriculum evaluation is that developed by Besco (1950), who looked at interests, needs, and abilities in a high school literature program and developed or adopted measures for each of these areas. Unfortunately, his analysis was brief, and he did not intercorrelate scores among the three. Smith and Tyler, Besco, Dressel and Mayhew, and Purves (in Bloom, Hastings, and Madaus, 1971) might well be referred to as guides for evaluation, as might the combined evaluations of the Program English projects.

Smaller studies have investigated curricular variations: Taylor found that high school literary types courses produced higher scores in literary interpretation than did topical courses, but no significant difference in reading comprehension or literary appreci-ation (taste). Unfortunately, this is only one of a few controlled curricular experiments we could find. O'Neill, Kamerman, and Chartrand (1969) found a college course in literature and social studies effective in dealing with prejudiced students in college. Some studies have tested the efficacy of a course without any control group, finding gain in either literary appreciation (Crabtree, 1932, inter al.) or general verbal skills (Murphy, 1964).

Three studies should be singled out because they are evaluations of Program English (originally Project English) curricula. Most of the curricula developed under that aegis contained little formal evaluation of the students' learning, although one did undertake a brief evaluation (Lazarus, 1967). Three of the projects, however, developed measures. The evaluation done at the Florida State University is perhaps the most elaborate, because evaluation was the primary concern (Burton et al., 1968). Designed to compare the efficacy of three junior high school programs—a language, literature, and writing approach, a thematic approach, and a cognitive processes approach—the team developed a multiple-choice poetry reading test, a multiple-choice short story reading test, a free response to a short story, a free response to a poem, and a semantic differential appraisal of the curriculum and the teachers. The free responses were coded according to the Squire categories with some modifications such as an added "unity response." The analysis of variance showed no significant difference between curricula on the poetry test, on the short story test, or on the semantic differential, except that the students found the thematic curriculum less complex than the cognitive processes curriculum. With respect to the free responses to the short story, students in the thematic and cognitive processes curriculum made fewer literary judgments and more interpretational responses. The students in the tripartite curriculum made more value judgments and literary judgments about poetry; those in the thematic curriculum, more paraphrases and abstract interpretations; and those in the cognitive processes curriculum, more self-involvement responses. This aspect of the study is partly confirmed by Sanders (1970). In general, however, the study shows that schools and teachers tend to account for more of the variance than does the curricular strategy.

Two other projects included elaborate evaluation. The Carnegie-Mellon project (Steinberg et al., 1968) tested a thematic and rhetorical literature program for able college-bound students, using several fascinating measures: a literary discernment test which used multiple-choice questions concerning ability in understanding, in detecting the entertainment, in comprehending the craft, and in comprehending the plot or theme of a selection; a literary preference questionnaire in which a student was asked his preference among comments concerning facts, entertaining features, the writer's craft, and the plot or theme of a work; a semantic differential; and a measure asking for preferred topics. There were significant differences in favor of the experimental program on only one measure, the literary discernment test. A later study, using informal measures, found the curriculum to be effective with average students, although some modification in quantity of reading was necessary (Slack, 1967).

The last of the Program English curriculum evaluations is that of Fader and McNeil (1968) for the popular "Hooked on Books" project, also called "English in Every Classroom." This was a program designed to encourage free reading and free writing and thus improve the skills and attitudes of disadvantaged youth. The measures included a poetry sheet on which to record teachers' impressions of students' character and behavior; another to give teachers' impressions of students' attitudes, self-worth, attention span, and the like; students' attitude scales; students' self-ratings of behavior scales; students' classroom attitudes and literary attitudes; and verbal proficiency measures. Few significant differences between the experimental and control groups were found on these measures. The students in the experimental group decreased in anxiety, increased in self-esteem, and increased in esteem for their own literary efforts and in their general attitudes toward the printed word. Throughout all of these findings, however, runs a clear indication that a stronger differential than that of experimental or control is that of white and black children. In general the white students improved more than the black; such was particularly true on the teacher questionnaires and measures of the students' self-image and attitude toward education, in which the nonwhite student comes off poorly. In the literature measures this difference tends to disappear.

Each of these curriculum projects (Florida State, Carnegie-Mellon, and "English in Every Classroom") reflects an important advance in the technology of curriculum evaluation. If these measures were pooled, there would exist a substantial and effective criterion measure for curriculum evaluation. It is to be hoped that future projects will make use of these measures.

One last aspect of curriculum evaluation needs to be mentioned—the curriculum survey. Several have been undertaken from time to time, each seeking to find out what is being taught and how it is done. Despite the value of local studies like those of Eisenman (1962), Whitworth (1964), Conner (1966), and Rickard (1967), for our purposes the most useful are those of Hahn (1968), Anderson (1964), and Squire and Applebee (1968). Hahn classified accounts of successful teachers, finding independent reading programs and genre studies most successful. The major emphasis of these teachers was on literature as experience (50 percent), as exemplification of form (31 percent), as theme (10 percent), and as standard corpus (9 percent). Anderson, who sought to find out what major works were most commonly taught, found that no work was universally taught and that *Macbeth*, taught in 75 percent of the schools, was most popular. The next leading work was taught in only about 50 percent of the schools, a clear indication of the increasing diversity of the curriculum. Squire and Applebee surveyed 116 highly rated schools and 42 others (experimental, parochial, private, and comprehensive). Among their findings are these: literature occupies 52.2 percent of curricular time; there is no consensus about the objectives of teaching literature; there is no consensus about approach, although the prevailing pattern was thematic or typological study in grades nine and ten, American literature in grade eleven, and British or world literature in grade twelve; students' most significant reading is not the literature taught; and, in general, literature teaching is the strong point of the schools. Squire and Applebee's later study of selected British schools (1970) found quite a different curricular emphasis (much more attention to writing) as well as different texts and approaches.

D. Extensive Reading

One curriculum practice has been well studied, and the results of each study tend to confirm the others. The practice is that of comparing "the rapid reading of a comparatively large number of literary works with general comments and discussions in class" (the extensive method) with "the detailed analytical study of the minimum of literary works" (the intensive method) (Coryell, 1927). Coryell made the first and most elaborate study in 1927, testing the two groups and a control group on five of the works commonly taught by both methods. For each work objectives were drawn up, and the most important were measured by objective tests and by a scoring of stenographic reports of classes. Only one significant difference was found: that in favor of the middle-level students taught in the extensive manner. Other measures of reading, word knowledge, and general literary achievement were administered again with no significant differences between groups.

Coryell's study has been confirmed by Smith (1941), Morsey (1961), Terry (1965), and Fader and McNeil (1968). The one dissenting voice is that of Wyatt (1960), who found that extensive reading does not affect writing or other language skills with the exception of spelling. Her study suggests that other measures—measures like the style of response measures of Squire and others—might be used to judge the differences between these seemingly radically different curricula.

E. Individualized Reading Programs

While distinctions between extensive reading programs and more recent programs, such as individualized reading, free reading, or personalized reading, are blurred in the research, these latter programs are concerned less with achievement gain and more with developing interests in and attitudes toward literature.

Studies indicate that development of reading skills and imposition of teachers' attitudes have received priority over development of students' interests and attitudes (Stanchfield, 1960; Ruth Smith, 1962; Barbe, 1963). When students were allowed self-selection, interest in reading and amount of voluntary reading increased. Students showed a decrease in interest in reading required selections (Green, 1923; Washburne and Vogel, 1926; LaBrant and Heller, 1939).

An essential aspect of the individualized program is that of unrestricted self-selection of reading material (Rinehart, 1931; Rothney and McCaul, 1938; Wagner, 1952). An early survey (Stroh, 1926) found that students had little choice in book selection. Even today, 90 percent of the professors in colleges never allow student selection, usually citing the students' inexperience (Logan, 1972).

Studies of the effects of free-reading programs vary in quality. The fact that all those conducted in the thirties (Beggs, 1931; Adams, 1933; Royster, 1933; Persing and Sattley, 1935; LaBrant and Heller, 1939) found gains in interest has led some persons to be suspicious of philosophical biases. None of these was an experimental study. However, a number of later experimental studies have confirmed these earlier findings. Norvell (1950) matched 24 free-reading classes with 24 more restrictive classes. Students and teachers preferred the free-reading program, and small but significant gains occurred in reading ability in the free-reading classes, as well as in the others. Hardwick (1970) compared a personalized reading program with a basal reading program and found that the personalized program produced equally significant gains in attitudes and skills. The advocate of free-reading programs should, however, temper his enthusiasm in the light of Bertha Handlan's (1946) article, which points to some fallacies in the approach.

A survey of 7000 students indicated a desire for more leisure reading in the school program (Fisk, 1961). Gallo (1968) found that students did not like book reports, enjoyed discussing books in small groups, and preferred group discussion to discussions led by the teacher.

In one of the few studies which related classroom variables to interests, Sauls (1971) found no significant relationship between the teacher's attitude toward recreational reading and the amount read by students. However, a significant relationship did occur between the teacher's score on a checklist describing promotional practices for encouraging voluntary reading and the amount read by students of that teacher.

In a study comparing the effects of teachers' and parents' efforts to work with reluctant readers to help them develop a positive commitment to independent reading, Schmidt (1970) concluded that a concerted effort by both teachers and parents was needed in order to bring about improvement. He found that while IQ and reading ability are correlated with self-commitment to reading, they are not such significant factors that they cannot be overcome by home and school literary environments which encourage independent reading.

Appleby (1967) examined the kinds of effects that resulted from an individualized program. While no significant differences were found on standardized tests of satisfaction from reading, differences were found favoring the individualized program in reading fiction for self-development, reading fiction for information, and in developing fewer dislikes of fiction.

More careful research, in which particular instructional variables, if any, in an individualized reading program enhance certain interests, would shed light on the larger movement toward more informal classroom approaches.

F. Instrumental Uses of Literature

Only a few studies exist dealing with the interrelation of literature and other language skills, some of which are peripheral. Mills

(1967) tried using literary models for writing rhetorical tropes and found them successful with eighth grade children. Two studies dealt with sixth graders' understanding of figurative language (Simmons, 1954; Horne, 1966). Both found the students had difficulty understanding figurative language; Simmons found two lessons insufficient to effect improvement; and Horne found 24 sufficient. Horne's, the better study of the two, also found that experience is a more important factor in understanding figurative language than age or reading ability.

Except for Wyatt's (1960) study, the only study of actual instrumental effect is that of Cohen (1968), who found that reading literature aloud to second grade disadvantaged youth every day had a significant effect in improving vocabulary (.005), word knowledge (.005), and reading comprehension (.01). With the very lowest classes, the differences were significant at the .05 level. Cohen's study is certainly important for the education of young children; whether the effect persists with older children is moot, although many of the studies note gain in reading comprehension scores as a result of literature programs or classes no matter what form the programs or classes take (Knapp, 1960; Monson, 1968; Murphy, 1969).

G. Studies Dealing with Teachers and Teacher Training

In addition to the curriculum survey studies mentioned above, all of which tell us about the attitudes, experience, and methods of literature teachers, there are a few which speak specifically to teacher competence, attitude, and training. Those of Ahrens (1965) and Katz (1968) describe teachers' experience with and perception of censorship in the schools. It is perceived as a real threat, the threat coming most often from parents and students who object to language and incidents they deem improper.

Four studies deal with teacher competencies and are important for those engaged in preservice training. Madsen (1968) reviewed prospective teachers' deficiencies in literary criticism, particularly in the knowledge of the terminology and theory of the "new critics," the Fryean critics, and the Chicago School. Ducharme (1967) found that prospective teachers were deficient in the ability to read an unfamiliar text. Braddock and Mittman (1962) discovered that this deficiency was especially strong in the interpretation of an ironic selection. Miller (1969) found that junior high school teachers needed to develop competence in the knowledge of children's books, in the motivation of children, in children's interests and literary tastes. Unfortunately, Miller could find no clear correlation between these competencies and students' enjoyment of reading. A study that goes beyond knowledge to action is that of Davidson (1967), who found that, by developing an interaction system focused on children's critical thinking and providing feedback to teachers on their influence on such thinking, he could modify that influence. Obviously more studies of this type need to be undertaken, for by this sort of connection between teacher behavior and pupil behavior, development of appropriate teacher competencies may be forthcoming.

One major step forward in this area is the study of Gallo (1968), who first constructed an instrument to gather teachers' opinions about teaching poetry and then validated the instrument against the attitudes, personality, performance, and success of the teachers in teaching poetry to average tenth graders. The measure proved reliable, but its correlation with tapes of teachers' performance and with student performance was tenuous. Despite the partial failure in this attempt, the attempt should be repeated, particularly to develop a diagnostic measure for prospective teachers, similar to the measures developed for the Illinois Statewide Curriculum Study Center in the Preparation of English Teachers (ISCPET) by Hook, Jacobs, and Crisp (1969). That profession and practice are not correlated is a serious problem and a recurrent one, but its recognition can get us well on the way to developing definitive statements of teacher competence.

A final type of study should be noted. The first is Bragle's review in 1969 of the College Entrance Examination Board Summer Institutes, which dealt with language, literature, and writing. This was a follow-up study three years after the institutes. The teacher-participants reported that they were still using many of the materials. Perhaps they were trying to please the researcher, but one wonders whether they should not have gone beyond those institutes. The second series of studies are those of ISCPET, which coordinated studies in English education and prepared lists of teacher qualifications, references, and training programs. Its contribution most germane to this study was the development of a series of tests and scales, including one in literature, which measured the literary knowledge and critical ability of prospective teachers. The tests in literature are not as effective, perhaps, as those in composition, but they are certainly as good as the National Teacher Examination.

Summary

As we said at the beginning of this chapter, studies of classroom or curricular treatment with respect to literature are not many, but what few there are point to certain specific areas for future investigation.

The first is the investigation of what the teacher does. "Teaching" literature, intervening in the natural response processes of young people, seems to have an effect on them, on their cognitive performance, on their attitudes, and perhaps on their interest patterns. This sort of intervention seems to have more effect than does the manipulation of the material taught or of the structure and sequence of material. The nature and effects of different kinds of intervention need to be explored, particularly the relation between the type of intervention and the kinds of outcomes that are sought or measured. The studies seem to have shown that more open kinds of teaching lead toward diversity among the students, more closed kinds, toward singularity. This finding, however, is questionable simply because the measures and the teaching have been too closely linked.

This criticism leads to the second area, that of applying multiple measures to single treatment variables. Most of the studies have used only one or, at best, a handful of measures. Yet, as the studies themselves (and the first two chapters of this review of research) have indicated, there is a multiplicity of facets of literary achievement. A treatment variable may not affect one of those facets, but it may affect others. Comprehensive measurement might well show differences where few or none had appeared with single measures.

The only sure evidence we have of the efficacy of any variable is that related to extensive reading. The studies generally confirm that extensive reading is as effective as intensive reading in certain ways, particularly as regards critical reading achievement and attitude. Whether or not there is an effect on the pattern of response is yet unknown.

A fourth area of concern deals with the polycultural aspect of our society and the diversity of cultural literatures. The studies seem to indicate that when students see a relation or "relevance" to literature they will perform better. Certainly, however, many studies related to ethnic literatures and the response patterns and achievements that emerge from the teaching of these literatures might well be undertaken. Not only should these studies deal with a group reading its own literature but with a group reading the literature of other groups. Certainly more studies should deal with nonreaders or speakers of dialectical variants.

Finally, much more needs to be done in studying the incidental effects of teaching literature. What are its instrumentalities as regards the general linguistic development of the individual, as regards his perceptions and conceptions, as regards his responses to the other arts and the sciences? What are its impacts on the teaching and learning of literature? These are but a few questions, large ones, to be sure, but ones to which researchers may well pay attention, perhaps, as we said earlier, through other modes of research than the experimental or the large-group survey. The anthropological and psychoanalytic studies provide possible guides.

Bibliography

Ahrens, Nyla H. "Censorship and the Teacher of English: A Questionnaire Survey of a Selected Sample of Secondary School Teachers of English." Diss. Teachers College, Columbia University, 1965.

Alm, Richard S. "A Study of Assumptions Concerning Human Experience Underlying Certain Works of Fiction." Diss. University of Minnesota, 1954.

Anderson, O. "The Significance of Profundity in Literary Appreciation." *The Reading Research Quarterly* 5 (1969), 100-118.

Anderson, Scarvia. *Between the Grimms and "The Group": Literature in American High Schools.* Princeton, New Jersey: Educational Testing Service, 1964.

Appleby, Bruce C. "The Effects of Individualized Reading on Certain Aspects of Literature Study with High School Seniors." Diss. University of Iowa, 1967.

Barbe, W. B. "Interests and the Teaching of Reading." *Education* 83 (1963), 486-490.

Beal, Elizabeth. "An Evaluation of Certain Children's Books on Human Relations in Terms of Literary Merit, Readability, Interests, and Other Psychological Values." Diss. Western Reserve University, 1963.

Becker, Samuel L., Rhodes Dunlap, and John C. Gerber. *A Comparison of Three Methods of Teaching Modern Literature.* Iowa City, Iowa: University of Iowa, 1957.

Bernard, Ida, Edna Anderson, and Susie Raburn. "A Reading

Course in Modern Literature." *California Quarterly of Secondary Education* 3 (January 1928), 133-138.

Besco, Galen S. "Interests, Needs, and Abilities as Factors in High School Literature Programs." Diss. Ohio State University, 1950.

Bloom, Benjamin, J. Thomas Hastings, and George Madaus. *Handbook of Formative and Summative Evaluation of Student Learning.* New York: McGraw-Hill, Inc., 1971.

Blount, Nathan S. "The Effect of Selected Junior Novels and Selected Adult Novels on Student Attitudes toward the 'Ideal' Novel." Diss. Florida State University, 1963.

_____. "The Effect of Selected Junior Novels and Selected Adult Novels on Student Attitudes toward the 'Ideal' Novel." *Journal of Educational Research* 59 (December 1965), 179-182.

Boehner, Grace A. "College Life Problems as an Introduction to Masterpieces of Literature." Diss. Teachers College, Columbia University, 1946.

Braddock, Richard R. "Group Reading of Novels." Diss. Teachers College, Columbia University, 1952.

Braddock, Richard R., and Arthur Mittman. "Can We Tell How Much They Know? A Report on the Iowa Pilot Study of the NCTE Teacher-Exam Project." *Iowa English Yearbook* 7 (1962), 45-52.

Bragle, George W. "An Evaluation of the 1962 CEEB Workshops in New York State." Diss. State University of New York at Albany, 1969.

Bridge, Ethel B. "Using Children's Choices of and Reactions to Poetry as Determinants in Enriching Literary Experience in the Middle Grades." Diss. Temple University, 1966.

Broening, Angela M. *Developing Appreciation through Teaching Literature.* The Johns Hopkins University Studies in Education, no. 13. Baltimore, Maryland: The Johns Hopkins Press, 1929.

Brownell, John, Connie Meredith, and Anne Nicol. *Final Evaluation of the 1967 Summer Experimental Program of the Hawaii Curriculum Center*. Honolulu, Hawaii: Hawaii Curriculum Center, 1967.

Burch, Mary C. "Determination of a Content of the Course in Literature of a Suitable Difficulty for Junior and Senior High School Students." *Genetic Psychology Monographs*, vol. 4, nos. 2 and 3 (1928).

Burress, Lee A. *How Censorship Affects the School*. Special Bulletin, no. 8, Wisconsin Council of Teachers of English. Stevens Point, Wisconsin: Wisconsin State College, 1963.

Burton, Dwight L. *The Development and Testing of Approaches to Teaching of English in the Junior High School*. Report at Florida State University, June 30, 1968. Final Report Project No. H-026, Contract No. OE-4-10-018.

――――. "An Experiment in Teaching Appreciation of Fiction." *English Journal* 42 (January 1953), 16-20.

Cohen, Dorothy H. "Effect of a Special Program in Literature on the Vocabulary and Reading Achievement of Second Grade Children in Special Service Schools." Diss. New York University, 1966.

――――. "The Effect of Literature on Vocabulary and Reading Achievement." *Elementary English* 45 (February 1968), 209-213, 217.

Compere, Moiree S. "Studies in the Teaching of Poetry." Diss. Michigan State College, 1952.

Conner, John W. "Practices in Teaching Literature in Representative Public Four-Year Iowa High School Districts." Diss. University of Iowa, 1966.

Coryell, Nancy G. "An Evaluation of Extensive and Intensive Teaching of Literature." *Teachers College Contributions to Edu-*

cation, no. 175. New York: Bureau of Publications, Teachers College, Columbia University, 1927.

Crabtree, Eunice K. *A Study of the Effect of a Course in Children's Literature upon Students' Own Literary Appreciation Experimentally Determined in a Normal School.* Washington, D.C.: Judd and Detweiler, Inc., 1932.

Crawford, Elizabeth M. "Achievement of Secondary School Pupils in Twelve Classics in Literature." *Teachers College Journal* (Indiana State Teachers College) 10, no. 2 (1938), 21-40.

Curtis, Alice, et al. *Reading for the Gifted—Guided Extension of Reading Skills through Literature: Part I, Appreciating the Contributions of One Author.* Los Angeles, California: Los Angeles City Schools, 1966.

D'Annunzio, Anthony. "An Investigation of the Effects of Three Different Reading Programs on Junior High School Students." Diss. Temple University, 1965.

Danielson, Cora L. "A Study of the Effect of a Definite Course of Reading in General Literature upon Achievement in Content Subjects with Children of Superior Mental Ability." *Journal of Educational Psychology* 20 (November 1929), 610-621.

Davidson, Roscoe L. "The Effects of an Interaction Analysis System on the Development of Critical Reading in Elementary School Children." Diss. University of Denver, 1967.

Dressell, Paul L., and Lewis D. Mayhew. *General Education: Explorations in Evaluation.* Washington, D.C.: American Council on Education, 1954.

Ducharme, Edward R. "Close Reading and the Teaching of Poetry in English Education and in Secondary Schools." Diss. Teachers College, Columbia University, 1967.

Eisenman, Sister Mary Victoria. "An Exploratory Study to Investigate the Values of Literature as Experienced by Elementary

Parochial School Children and Teachers in the Diocese of Covington." Diss. St. Louis University, 1962.

Fader, Daniel N. *English for Reluctant Learners, Grades Seven through Nine: English in Every Classroom.* University of Michigan, 1966.

Fader, Daniel N., and Elton B. McNeil. *Hooked on Books: Program and Proof.* New York: G. P. Putnam's Sons, 1968.

Fisk, Robert. "A Survey of Leisure Reading in the Junior High Schools of Alberta." Diss. University of Alberta, 1961.

Foster, Jeannette H. "An Approach to Fiction through the Characteristics of Its Readers." *The Library Quarterly* 6 (April 1936), 124-174.

Fox, Maude G. "An Experiment in Promoting Interest in Reading." *Elementary School Journal* 46 (April 1947), 451-460.

Gallo, Donald R. "The Construction and Validation of an Instrument to Assess Teachers' Opinions of Methods of Teaching Poetry to Tenth Grade Students of Average Ability." Diss. Syracuse University, 1968.

Gershenfeld, Howard. "A Guidance Approach to Reading at the Junior High School Level." Diss. Teachers College, Columbia University, 1958.

Glenn, Robert. "Relating the Subcultural World of the Teenager to Literature." Diss. United States International University, 1968.

Green, J. L. "When Children Read for Fun." *School and Society* 17 (1923), 390-392.

Grindstaff, Faye L. "The Responses of Tenth Grade Students to Four Novels." Diss. Colorado State College, 1968.

Hackett, Marie G., George I. Brown, and William Michael. "A Study of Two Strategies in the Teaching of Literature in the

Secondary School." *School Review* (University of Chicago) **76** (March 1968), 67-83.

Hahn, Elizabeth C. L. "Critical Emphasis Revealed in Selected Practices in Literature Instruction in the Public Secondary School." Diss. University of Connecticut, 1968.

Hand, Harry E. "Modern Novels in Senior High School English: A Study Concerning Practices and Opinions of Teachers of High School English in the State of Michigan." Diss. University of Michigan, 1959.

Handlan, Bertha. "The Fallacy of Free Reading as an Approach to Appreciation." *English Journal* 35 (April 1946), 182-188.

Hardwick, Louise. "The Effect of a Personalized Reading Program on the Reading Skills, Attitudes, Study Habits, and Self-Concepts of Seventh Grade Students." Diss. University of California at Los Angeles, 1970.

Hillocks, George, Jr. *An Evaluation of Project APEX: A Non-graded Phase-Elective English Program.* Trenton, Michigan: Trenton Public Schools, 1971.

————. *Questioning Processes in the Teaching of Literature: A Proposal for Research.* Bowling Green, Ohio: Bowling Green State University, n.d.

Hoetker, James. *Students as Audiences: An Experimental Study of the Relationships between Classroom Study of Drama and Attendance at the Theatre.* NCTE Research Report, no. 11. Urbana, Illinois: National Council of Teachers of English, 1971.

————. "Teacher Questioning Behavior in Nine Junior High School English Classes." *Research in the Teaching of English* 2 (1968), 99-106.

Hoetker, James, and W. P. Ahlbrand. "The Persistence of the Recitation." *American Educational Research Journal* (March 1969), 145-167.

Hogue, Bradley B., Jr. "Some Effects of a Reader Written for Children of Low Socioeconomic Circumstances." Diss. North Texas State University, 1964.

Hook, J. N., Paul Jacobs, and Raymond Crisp. *Illinois State-Wide Curriculum Study in the Preparation of Secondary English Teachers: Final Report*. Urbana, Illinois: University of Illinois, 1969.

Horne, Rose N. "A Study of the Use of Figurative Language by Sixth Grade Children." Diss. University of Georgia, 1966.

Katz, John. "Controversial Novels and Censorship in the Schools." Diss. Harvard University, 1968.

Kay, Muriel M. "An Examination of Some Psychology Effects of Teaching English in Schools." *Educational Research* 2 (February 1960), 149-151.

King, Martha, et al. *Observations of Teacher-Pupil Verbal Behavior during Critical Reading Lessons*. Columbus, Ohio: Ohio State University, 1967.

Klausmeier, Herbert J. *Individualizing Instruction in Language Arts through Development and Research in Research and Instructional Units of Local Schools*. Madison, Wisconsin: University of Wisconsin, 1967.

Knapp, Edgar H. "Effects of Various Approaches upon Poetry Comprehension of High School Sophomores." Diss. Teachers College, Columbia University, 1960.

Koob, Theodora J. "Determination of the Effect of Teaching Literature with Emphasis upon Individual Interpretation of Figurative Language." Diss. New York University, 1946.

LaBrant, Lou L., and F. M. Heller. "An Evaluation of Free Reading in Grades Seven to Twelve Inclusive." *Contributions to Education*, no. 4. Columbus, Ohio: Ohio State University Press, 1939.

LaRocque, G. E. "The Effectiveness of the Inductive and Deductive

Methods of Teaching Figurative Language to Eighth Grade Students." Diss. Stanford University, 1965.

Lazarus, Arnold. *The Report on Project English at Purdue: Response of 4000 Midwestern Seventh Graders to Twelve Literary Works.* Lafayette, Indiana: Purdue Research Foundation, 1967.

Lemmons, William E., R. Dubose LaRocque, Kenneth W. Hirsch, and Donald R. Stevens. *Report of the Committee for the Study of the Mass Lecture Method of Teaching College Freshman English Courses.* Bozeman, Montana: Montana State University, 1966.

Leopold, Kathleen B. "The Effects of Creative Work on Aesthetic Appreciation." *British Journal of Educational Psychology* 3 (1933), 42-50.

Levinson, Elias. *Effects of Motion Pictures on the Response to Narrative.* Diss. New York University, 1962.

Livingston, H. "The Effects of General Semantics on Responses to a Poem." *Research in the Teaching of English* 3 (1969), 25-29.

Logan, Chester. "What Students and Faculty Read." *Change* 4 (May 1972), 10-11.

Madsen, Alan L. *Responses of Prospective English Teachers to a Test on Theories of Literary Criticism.* Urbana, Illinois: University of Illinois, 1968.

Miller, Lewis J. "Fostering Interest in Children's Literature: Selected Teachers' Practices and Competencies." Diss. Indiana University, 1969.

Mills, Edith B. "An Experimental Study in the Use of Literary Models in Written Composition." Diss. University of Georgia at Athens, 1967.

Monson, Dianne L. "Influence of Method of Questioning upon Children's Responses to Humorous Situations in Literature." Paper delivered at the annual meeting of the American Educational Research Association, February 1968.

Morris, Claire E. "A Study of the Differential Effectiveness of a Preplanned-Sequentially Structured Approach and an Incidental Unstructured Approach upon the Appreciation of Literature of Sixth Grade Pupils." Diss. University of Pennsylvania, 1970.

Morsey, Royal J. *A College Seminar to Develop and Evaluate an Improved High School English Program*. Muncie, Indiana: Ball State University, 1961.

Murphy, Morris. "Compensatory Education I and II: Profile of an Interdisciplinary Program." *Research in Education* 4 (May 1969), 59. (Resumé only.)

Nesmith, Mary E. "An Objective Determination of Stories and Poems for the Primary Grades." *Teachers College Contributions to Education*, no. 255. New York: Bureau of Publications, Teachers College, Columbia University, 1927.

Neumeyer, Peter F. "A Structural Approach to the Study of Literature for Children." Diss. Harvard University, 1966.

Norvell, George W. *The Reading Interests of Young People*. Boston, Massachusetts: D. C. Heath and Company, 1950.

O'Neill, John H. "Report on Offerings of the Sixteen-Credit Course, Problems in Contemporary Race Relations, Fall 1968, and Winter 1969." *The General College Studies* 6, no. 1 (1969-1970).

O'Neill, John H., Jack Kamerman, and William R. Chartrand. "Interim Report on the Sixteen-Credit Combined Course Offered in the General College, Spring Quarter 1969." *The General College Studies* 5, no. 1 (1968-1969).

Parsons, Paul J. "A Modern Broad Context Approach to the Study and Teaching of Literature." Diss. Colorado University Teachers College, 1960.

Prettyman, E. P. "Two Methods of Teaching English Literature and Student Attitudes toward These Methods." Diss. Pennsylvania State University, 1965.

Purkey, William W. *The Preparation and Evaluation of an Experimental Independent Study Program for Gifted High School Under-Achievers.* Gainesville, Florida: University of Florida, 1967.

Rickards, Montana H. "A Study of Newer Programs and Trends in the Teaching of Literature in Selected Oregon Senior High Schools." Diss. University of Oregon, 1967.

Rinehart, Anne C. "What Pittsburgh High School Students Read." *School Betterment Studies* 2, no. 1 (1930), 9-83.

————. "What Pittsburgh Junior High School Pupils Read." *School Betterment Studies* 3, no. 1 (1931), 84.

Roberts, Mary V. "Understanding of Allusions Possessed by Ninth Grade Students." Diss. University of Missouri, 1967.

Rosen, Carl L., and Philip D. Ortego. *Problems and Strategies in Teaching the Language Arts to Spanish-Speaking Mexican-American Children.* Las Cruces, New Mexico: New Mexico State University, 1969.

Rothney, John, and Robert McCaul. "Reading Preferences of High School Boys." *English Journal* 27 (October 1938), 650-660.

Ruhlen, Helen V. "Experiment in Testing Appreciation." *English Journal* 25 (1926), 202-209.

Sanders, Peter L. "An Investigation of the Effects of Instruction in the Interpretation of Literature on the Responses of Adolescents to Selected Short Stories." Diss. Syracuse University, 1970.

Sauls, Charles W. "The Relationship of Selected Factors to the Recreational Reading of Sixth Grade Students." Diss. Louisiana State University, 1971.

Schmidt, Sheldon L. "A Study of the Development of Self-Commitment to Independent Reading in Uncommitted Fourth Grade Students." Diss. University of North Dakota, 1970.

Sherwin, Joseph S. "Social and Psychological Assumptions about Human Behavior in Selected Literary Works: An Analysis of the Literature at Present Required Reading in a Selected Secondary School and the Implications of the Analysis for the Improvement of Instruction in Literature." Diss. New York University, 1954.

Simmons, Lisso R. "An Experimental Study to Try to Improve the Ability of Sixth Grade Pupils to Interpret Metaphors Found in Their World History Textbook." Diss. Colorado State College at Greeley, 1954.

Slack, Robert C. *Program to Extend Curriculum Materials in English for the Able to a Wider Student Group.* Pittsburgh, Pennsylvania: Carnegie-Mellon University, 1967.

Smiley, Marjorie B. "Intercultural Education in English Classrooms: An Informal Survey." *English Journal* 35 (June 1946), 337-349.

Smith, Dora V. *Evaluating Instruction in Secondary School English: A Report of a Division of the New York Regents' Inquiring into the Character and Cost of Public Education in New York.* Urbana, Illinois: National Council of Teachers of English, 1941.

Smith, Eugene R., Ralph W. Tyler, and Evaluation Staff. *Appraising and Recording Student Progress. Adventure in American Education,* 3. New York: Harper and Brothers, 1942.

Smith, R. J. *The Effects of Reading a Short Story for a Creative Purpose on Student Attitudes and Writing: Technical Report No. 28.* Madison: University of Wisconsin, Wisconsin Research and Development Center for Cognitive Learning, 1967.

_____. "Effect of Reading for a Creative Purpose on Student Attitudes toward a Short Story." *Research in the Teaching of English* 2 (1968), 141-151.

Smith, Ruth C. "Children's Reading Choices and Basic Reader Content." *Elementary English* 39 (March 1962), 202-209.

Squire, James R., and Roger Applebee. *High School English Instruction Today: The National Study of High School English Programs*. New York: Appleton-Century-Crofts, 1968.

_____. *Teaching English in the United Kingdom: A Comparative Study*. Urbana, Illinois: National Council of Teachers of English, 1969.

Stanchfield, Jo Martha C. "A Study of Boys' Reading Interests in Relationship to Reading Achievement." Diss. University of California, 1960.

_____. "Boys' Reading Interests as Revealed through Personal Conferences." *Reading Teacher* 16 (September 1962), 41-44.

Steinberg, Erwin, et al. *A Senior High Curriculum in English for Able College-Bound Students*. Vol. 5, Summary Report. Pittsburgh, Pennsylvania: Carnegie-Mellon University, 1968. Available through ERIC (ED 011 966; EDRS price: microfiche-$.65, hard copy-$6.58, 111 p. Write ERIC Document Reproduction Service, P.O. Box 0, Bethesda, Maryland 20014).

Tatara, Walter T. "The Effect of a Supplementary Reading Program of Selected Fiction about the Scientist on Senior High School Students." Diss. New York University, 1962.

Taylor, Ruth E. "A Comparison of the Outcomes of Two Instructional Arrangements in High School Literature: The Topical Unit and the Literary Types." Diss. Indiana University, 1962.

Telford, J. P. "A Comparison of Student Response to a Collection of Original Stories, Poetry, and Discussion Lessons." Diss. Wayne State University, 1968.

Terrey, John N. "An Experiment Comparing Close Study and Wide Reading as Factors Contributing to an Ability to Judge Merit in Poetry." Diss. Washington State University, 1965.

Vergara, Allys D. "A Critical Study of a Group of College Women's Responses to Poetry." *Teachers College Contributions to*

Education, no. 923. New York: Bureau of Publications, Teachers College, Columbia University, 1946.

Wagner, Martha. "College Students Evaluate High School Reading." *English Journal* 41 (May 1952), 251-253.

Washburn, Carlton C. "Individualized Plan of Instruction in Winnetka." *Adjusting Reading Programs to Individuals.* Edited by William S. Gray, pp. 90-95. Supplementary Educational Monographs, no. 52. Chicago, Illinois: University of Chicago Press, 1941.

Washburne, C. W., and M. Vogel. *What Children Like to Read: The Winnetka Graded Book List.* Chicago, Illinois: American Library Association, 1926.

Weiss, James D. "The Relative Effects upon High School Students of Inductive and Programmed Instruction in the Close Reading of Poetry." Diss. New York University, 1968.

Whitworth, Richard G. "An Appraisal of the Problems Experienced by and the Techniques Used by English Teachers in Indianapolis, Indiana, Secondary Schools in Improving Student Reading Tastes." Diss. Indiana University, 1964.

Willis, Margaret. *The Guinea Pigs after Twenty Years.* Columbus, Ohio: Ohio State University Press, 1961.

Wilson, James R. *Responses of College Freshmen to Three Novels.* Diss. University of California at Berkeley, 1963.

Wyatt, Nita M. "A Study of the Relationships of Extensive Reading to Certain Writing Skills of a Selected Group of Sixth Grade Children." Diss. University of Kansas, 1960.

Conclusions and Implications

1. During the past fifty years, researchers have slowly dissected the complex phenomenon which is response to literature. They have shown that it contains cognitive aspects related to the ability to read and the possession of certain kinds of information as well as to the logical processes of thinking and of decoding complex messages. They have found that it consists of certain abilities to perceive sensuous aspects of language, particularly its sound and its image-making aspects, and that these abilities are only partially related to the cognitive ones. They have found that it consists of certain judgmental acts, which are based primarily upon liking or pleasure that the individual derives from the experience. They have found that a great deal of the "interference" or the difference between responses can be accounted for by the experiential, psychological, and conceptual baggage that the reader already has before picking up the book or scanning the poem. It is what the reader brings to the text as much as the text itself that determines the nature of the response. The model of literary response is quite different from an oversimple view of the communication model of *sender/message/receiver*. The reader takes as active a role in determining the message as does the sender.

2. The reasons for a reader reading and the satisfactions the reader derives from literature are many. The effects of literature upon readers are also many, and they are usually uncertain. One cannot predict that a certain poem or story will be approached by or will affect all readers in the same way. Too much of the effect is related to the reader and the circumstances of reading. At the same time, we know that a work of literature can have a profound effect

upon the beliefs and even upon the emotional life of the individual.

3. Over 35 years ago, Foster defined the average reader as feminine, 23.5 years old, possessing three years of high school education, reading three books every two weeks (generally light fiction, except for a nonfiction book and a "good" novel once a month), and taking most of her reading from the public library. That study has not been replicated, and one wonders whether it could be. We have come to recognize the diversity of our country, and we are only too aware that averages don't exist—in readers or in education. Yet studies in response to literature have looked much too little at differences among groups, when those groups are determined by something other than age, sex, or reading ability. We have barely begun to look at the responses of different ethnic groups, of groups differentiated on cognitive style, or of groups differentiated on geography or dialect.

4. In addition to being unclear as to the differences between people and the ties that bind them, we are still quite unaware of the relationships among the various aspects of response. Response consists of cognition, perception, and some emotional or attitudinal reaction; it involves predispositions; it changes during the course of reading; it persists and is modified after the work has been read; it may result in some overt action; and it may result in a modification of concepts, attitudes, or feelings. The research indicates that there may be some common processes, some sort of "kernels," from which the wide range of responses are generated. It may be that the process is so complex that one can never map the domain of response to literature fully, yet researchers should not give up the attempt. Continuing exploration will help curriculum builders and teachers better understand the articulations, or lack of them, of their students, better structure activities that enhance both cognitive and affective goals, and better define just what it is they want to teach.

5. The archetype of the some 360 studies on reading interests consists of a survey of titles students like and dislike, and from these preferences inferences are drawn that students are interested

in fiction, adventure, mystery, etc., that girls' interests differ from boys' interests, and that interests change with age. The major purpose for many such studies has been the establishment of reading lists. Scientific rigor was assumed unnecessary. Another purpose has been to establish norms of growth or "directionality," thereby assuming that behavioral indices (choosing one book over another) actually reflect students' interests. Few studies analyzed how different variables—availability, adults' perceptions of the child's interests, acculturation and socioeconomic determinants, instructional models, or media (singly or together)—influence reading interests. Almost none dealt with the relationship between the child's reading interests and his life style or other interests.

6. The problem of defining the concept *interest* has been ignored or, at best, skirted in many studies. Interests are not needs, drives, positive attitudes, or, in many cases, preferences. A student may prefer one book over another but be interested in neither. Merely checking likes or dislikes on a title checklist will not necessarily reveal interests—many students' interests have little to do with those titles available or familiar to them. In 1966 Getzels questioned the assumption behind his own definition of ten years earlier that interest is a tension-producing state which impels an individual to action, thus reducing the tension. His more positive assumption is that interests derive from a need to be stimulated rather than from the need for tension reduction. These two differing explanations of interest suggest alternative directions for research: the tension-reduction theory influences studies of the determinants which supposedly generate interests; and the need-for-stimulation theory suggests studies of the reader's reasons for loss of interest.

7. Related to this last point is the fact that there have been studies of interest, studies of taste, and studies of satisfaction, but neither these studies nor the studies of interest and response have been brought together. The wide-reading studies have dealt with cognitive outcomes, with one or two exceptions. Certainly there have been virtually no studies of the experimental nature in which

teaching or classroom variables have been introduced to affect interest.

8. In experimental studies, teacher-pupil interaction has generally been neglected, yet we know from the studies that have been made that that factor is the crucial one, accounting for nearly all of the variance in some cases. If we follow this finding through logically, we will abstain from treatment studies as unproductive, because they could tell us little that is generalizable beyond the particular class studied.

9. Aside from this finding, we do know that teaching literature, however teaching is defined, has an effect on the learner's performance. That is to say, we know that people can be trained to perform better on standardized literature tests and to perform in a divergent manner on tests that are more open in nature.

10. We do not know the side effects of the act of teaching literature. Most studies have used only a single measure of achievement or change. From the studies of response and effect, we know that literature is not single in its action on the individual. Any curricular or pedagogical treatment, therefore, has a multiplicity of effects—cognitive, aesthetic, and attitudinal. A worthwhile treatment study should take this multiplicity into account.

These ten areas of comment and question all point to the complexity of the process of reading literature and the need to show the interworkings of the process. We may say that literary response involves the following variables:

the reader—an individual's concepts, attitudes, and experiences, perceptual abilities, and emotional and psychological state;

the literary work—a verbal construct dealing with an experience and portrayed by a voice which reveals an attitude toward its subject matter and possible audience; and the situation of reading—whether assigned or not, whether in a classroom or not, whence and by whom stimulated, and for what purpose undertaken.

These three large groups of variables interact in starting the process of reading and responding which might or might not result in one of the following overt behaviors: stated responses of some sort— some verbal or nonverbal behavior which is an acknowledged result of the reading and response, which is communicable, and which may manifest itself up to several years after the experience of reading; or a modification of the reader's concepts, attitudes, perceptual abilities, and emotional or psychological state, which may not be an acknowledged result, may not be communicated, and may not be susceptible to measurement.

If this is the depiction of the process in large, we need to know more about the interactions of the three sets of variables both in process and in relation to the two possible results. Further, we need to know the effects of intervention on the result. We know something, but we do not know enough, and we certainly do not have sufficient evidence upon which to defend our curricular pronouncements. Obviously we will continue to make such pronouncements and continue to have curricula. Perhaps in the coming years, we will find evidence to guide our pronouncements and decisions.

Having made these pronouncements about the state of research and pointed out some areas for future research, what, in the meantime, can we say to the teacher? What has all this time, money, and energy done to help the teacher perform better? To begin at the end, we can say that the research indicates the importance of the teacher and of instruction (or at least of the structuring of learning situations) for the accomplishment of certain educational goals— development of critical reading, wider interests, and a wider critical repertoire. The structuring of those situations is, however, far from a cut and dried matter. The individual differences in blockages to understanding, in response patterns, in effects and satisfactions, in preconceptions and processes, and in preferences and interests are many—more than most curriculum makers would indicate. There are ways of finding out the individual style of a class or of students in a class; many of these ways are available to the teacher and of interest to the students. Questionnaires, opinion polls, cognitive preference tests, interviews, case studies—many of these are fascinating to young people (particularly in the secondary schools), whose curiosity about themselves is great, despite their reticence.

We would urge teachers to find out more about their students and to let their students into the research process. The joint exploration can be a stimulating endeavor. Besides the potential enjoyment of it, the teacher can acquire sufficient information to help choose materials, to help structure classes and exercises, and to help devise evaluative techniques. The function of research is to help in these basic pedagogical tasks. Knowing more about students and their transactions with literature can only enhance the effectiveness of the teacher.

Appendix: Summaries of Significant Studies

In making our review, we found ourselves returning to certain studies as touchstones for research in the teaching of literature. They are so for the information they have uncovered, for the answers they have given (although answers are often not too helpful), and for the importance of the questions they have raised. We admit that our judgment has been subjective, that it is not founded on any rigorous set of criteria save those of our best sense of the importance of the question, the adaptation of technique to the question asked, and the provocativeness of the solutions and partial answers. We seek to illustrate a variety of methods, not all of them statistical, and some of the statistical studies use techniques that have been superseded. A latter-day researcher should get behind the technique to the strategy. Some of the studies, like those abstracted here, have spawned other research; many have been virtually ignored.

Studies Dealing with the Nature of Literary Response.

Downey, June. *Creative Imagination: Studies in the Psychology of Literature.* London: Kegan, Paul, Trench, Trubner & Co., 1929. This volume reported the results of a number of small studies (mostly of secondary and college students) which have been detailed in other journals and monographs. Among the most pertinent was one dealing with the reactions of students to images. The reader was seen as tending to supply his own picture or background to an image. A second study dealt with the word-in-itself and the associations which individuals derive from words. These were classified into denotative, image-making, emotional, or word-in-itself visual or musical associations, the last dealing with physical appearance or cadence of the word. A third set of studies dealt with the self-projection of students into literary works and even images. People seem to have a kinaesthetic as well as a visual consciousness, and the projection might range from the detached or visual projection, through sympathetic or emotional projection, to empathetic or kinaesthetic projection. Another type of reader response was related to inner-speech. Readers tended to use one of four kinds: auditory (in which the reader heard his voice modified); auditory (in which the reader heard his own voice with strong motor quality); vocal motor (in which the reader's lips moved); and visual verbal (in which the reader "saw" words). All of these typologies served to point to a differentiation of types of responders to literature on the basis of physically or mentally active characteristics.

Richards, Ivor A. *Practical Criticism*. New York: Harcourt Brace, 1929.
This study gathered written responses to 13 poems from under-graduates and graduates at a British university. The responses were read and classified according to the difficulties in literary comprehension they evinced. The content analysis revealed ten factors: failure to make out the plain sense of the text, difficulty in sensuous apprehension, difficulty in visualizing imagery, mnemonic irrelevancies, stock responses, oversentimentality, overinhibition, doctrinal adhesion, technical presupposition, and general critical preconceptions. The study also isolated four characteristics of the work —sense, feeling, tone, and intention—which must be comprehended in order for the reader to make a valid critical assertion. Richards gives case study examples of responses to each of the texts and summarizes recommendations for teaching and criticizing.

Williams, E. D., L. Winter, and J. M. Woods. "Tests of Literary Appreciation." *British Journal of Educational Psychology*, 7 (1938), 265-284.

This study sought to measure the tastes of girls of different ages from 11 to 17 against a predetermined criterion, the tastes of adults. The measurement technique was the paired comparison, which the investigators found better for such a study than ranking, guessing the age of the writer, or a triple comparison. The intent of the study was to determine if any factor in judgment could be determined statistically. The team found the first factor to be one of general liking, which seemed related to the subject of the selection and its language. The second factor was a bipolar one related to technique (polished or mechanical, classical or romantic, or a similar term might define it). The judgments of children seemed slightly related to intelligence and slightly to age.

Strang, Ruth M. *Exploration in Reading Patterns*. Chicago, Illinois: University of Chicago Press, 1942.

The study involved an examination of the reading interests and abilities of 112 persons ranging in age from 13 to over 50 and representing various socioeconomic groups. The study consisted of a series of individual case studies with some generalizations about the characteristics of people's reading, their reading habits as related to the accessibility of material, reading interests and amount of rereading, and reading ability and general interests. The sample was not homogeneous in socioeconomic group or educational level, although a preponderance had graduated from high school or college. Among the findings was that the majority gave relaxation as a reason for reading, followed by the desire to learn something, self-improvement, knowledge about job, vicarious experience, and curiosity. In general, people chose books on the basis of interest in the subject, personal recommendation, convenience, and reviews. There were no single models or types of reader or interest, although some large and complex patterns appeared to emerge, patterns differentiating the highly verbal from those with low verbal ability. There was some relation between interest in the subject and enjoyment of what was read, estimation of difficulty, and proficiency in reading.

The author gathered some free responses to what had been read and found that the ability to write clearly about a work was not related to cognitive understanding of it but to expressive ability, and that the written expressions reflected the readers' experiences, emotions, and prejudices. From all the data emerged a conclusion that an individual's reading pattern has a central core or radix which determines its pattern.

Meckel, H. C. "An Exploratory Study of the Responses of Adolescent Pupils to Situations in a Novel." Dissertation. University of Chicago, 1946.

This study examined three questions: (1) To what situations in a novel did students respond most vividly? (2) What aspects of the novel did they prefer? and (3) What relationship occurred between personality predisposition and response to the novel? After reading each of four sections of the novel *Fortitude,* a story of a boy growing up, 96 high school seniors wrote a page of response about which situations impressed them. A free response test was administered at the completion of the novel, requesting students to list events more vividly remembered, to state preferences toward characters, plot, theme, and the novel as a whole, and to suggest any changes in the novel. Students were also asked to rate a prepared list of events in terms of how vividly events were remembered. Results were analyzed in terms of categories in the novel representing adolescent preoccupations: the relationship of the central character to himself, family, and peers; the love relationships; examples of aggressive behavior; and aids for the reader's philosophic outlook. Few situations from the novel were freely reported; free response listing tended to be highly individual. Students responded more to situations concerning parent-child and love relationships than to self-confrontation. Eighty-four percent of the responses reflected an identification between reader and other characters which was repressed due to personality predispositions caused by previous unpleasant experiences. Seventy-six percent of the responses were "personal-psychological"; 40.6 percent, content-ideational; 34.4 percent, technical-critical. The study concluded that the vicarious experience of identification reflects a strong value-orientation in reading of fiction.

Shrodes, Caroline. "Bibliotherapy: A Theoretical and Clinical Experimental Study." Dissertation. University of California at Berkeley, 1950.

This study explored the theory and practice of bibliotherapy, which is grounded on the theory that there is an integral relationship between the personality of the reader and the aesthetic experience of literature, particularly of literature as a psychological field. The process is one of identification, projection, catharsis, and insight, and it is manifest in the selective perception and report of the reader. The literature and discussion of it may modify the individual's cognitive organization. Shrodes performed an experimental study with college students, diagnosing the needs of students in the area of interpersonal relations, assigning readings, and securing detailed reactions to the reading. Few results of this were given, the bulk of the work devoted to a single case study of a woman who needed to reconcile conformity with self-respect. Books were selected and detailed responses were gathered and analyzed, showing a gradual move from ambivalence to objectivity about herself, although anxiety, guilt, and insecurity were always present. The diagnosis was related to other psychological tests (Rorschach, Maslow's Security-Insecurity Test, California Public Opinion Poll, Progressive Education Association Interest Inventory) and was found to be generally valid both internally and externally. Shrodes suggested several areas for further research of both an experimental and a case study nature.

Alpert, Harvey. "The Relationship of Empathy to Reading Comprehension in Selected Content Fields." Dissertation. University of Florida, 1955.

The study examined 101 university undergraduates in the light of six variables: empathy, projection, literary comprehension, nonliterary comprehension, intelligence, and adjustment. The following conclusions were reached: females scored significantly higher on the empathy test than did the males; empathy was not related to the ability to read literary materials or nonliterary materials (for women, empathy was related to poor reading ability); degree of projection was not related to sex or reading comprehension; for women, however, projection was positively correlated with literary comprehension and negatively correlated with comprehension of nonliterary materials. Alpert inferred that empathetic tendencies may hinder comprehension but that measures of the tendency to project one's feelings and attitudes are measuring emotional involvement and that this kind of involvement does enhance the comprehension of literature but not of factual materials. Measures of projection, therefore, can help predict the ability, particularly of women, to read literary works.

Carroll, John B. "Vectors of Prose Style." In *Style in Language,* edited by Thomas A. Sebeok. Cambridge and New York: Technology Press and John Wiley, 1960.
Carroll investigated the descriptions by eight expert judges of 150 prose passages as those descriptions were filtered through 29 adjectival scales. These scales were factor analyzed, producing six factors: stylistic evaluation, personal affect, ornamentation, abstractness, seriousness, and characterization. The scales proved reliable (.64 to .92), the least reliable being the evaluative scales, and the most reliable, the descriptive scales. The sixth descriptive factor was based on proportions of transitive verbs, copulative verbs, proper nouns, and adjective clauses. The study suggests a methodology for comparing and contrasting the evaluations of works and can be related to the studies of Hansson and of Williams, Winter, and Woods. Carroll's study needs to be viewed as a study of judgment as much as of style.

Hansson, Gunnar. *Dikt i Profil (Poetry in Profile)*. Göteborg, Sweden: Akademiforlaget-Gumperts, 1964.
The study examined the relationship of critical judgments to a reference-group of values to determine if there were group norms of response. The procedure was to ask three groups (university and college teachers of literature, first-year university students of literature, and adults with a high school education) to respond at twelve different points in a poem, using a series of bipolar seven-point scales. The profiles of response on the polar scales (e.g., tragic-happy, still-moving, fast-slow, quiet-unquiet) were similar for the three groups. The only differences were in those scales dealing with formal poetic qualities. The method served adequately to support the hypothesis that the process of response was similar for groups of different educational levels. The scales proved adequate, although Hansson refined them to produce unipolar scales.

Rosenblatt, Louise M. "The Poem as Event." *College English* 26 (November 1964), 123-128.
This article reported on a study in which a group of high school teachers of English read a brief poem and were asked to jot down whatever came into their heads during a period of 30 minutes. From an analysis of these jottings, the writer concluded that most readers were active in the sense of building up a poem for themselves from the lines and selecting referents for the symbols on the page. The readers were also egocentric in that they paid attention to what the poem evoked in them; at the same time, they were seeking an organizing principle. ". . . The reader's creation of a poem out of a text [was] a *self*-ordering and *self*-correcting process." The process was partly controlled by the text, which served as a "blueprint" for the response.

Squire, James R. "The Responses of Adolescents to Literature Involving Selected Experiences of Personal Development." Dissertation. University of California at Berkeley, 1956. (Partially reproduced in *The Responses of Adolescents while Reading Four Short Stories*. Urbana, Illinois: National Council of Teachers of English, 1964.)

Squire explored two areas: (1) the nature of responses to literary selections and (2) the reasons why individuals respond to literature in unique and selective ways. Four short stories focusing on episodes of personal development were presented to 52 fifteen-year-old readers, who responded orally to each story at six different points in the progress of the story. The investigator used content-analysis to develop categories for analyzing and coding the responses. Seven categories resulted: literary judgments, interpretational responses, narrational reactions, associational responses, self-involvement, prescriptive judgments, and miscellaneous. The main findings of the study can be listed as follows: readers responded to fiction in unique and selected ways; sex differences did not affect the overall pattern of adolescent response to fiction; readers who became deeply involved in a story were more likely to consider the literary values of the story; intelligence and reading measures did not predict the quality of individual interpretations of the stories; and there were very few associational responses, indicating that adolescents often failed to relate fiction to their own experiences. The study implied that adolescent readers need assistance in interpreting fiction, while reading as well as after reading, particularly to enable them to control emotional responses long enough to evaluate objective evidence; adolescents are inclined to "happiness binding." It also implied that teachers need to use better techniques, like the one in the study, and to evaluate response to literature, since standard intelligence and reading measures are not significantly related to interpretational ability.

Ennis, Philip. *Adult Book Reading in the United States*. Chicago, Illinois: National Opinion Research Center, 1965.

The study reported on the results of 18 in-depth interviews with adults in and out of school, both regular and irregular readers. The results described time spent reading, amount of books read, types read, reasons for reading in general and for reading specific types of books, sources of books, and many other topics. The major findings included a general tendency in people to read about what they want to believe—to read books that fit into their personal lives. They tend to develop strands of reading preference moving from one title to another dealing with the same topic or by the same author. The amount of reading depends on availability, on the existence of a circle of acquaintances who read, on income, and on education in a complex set of relationships. The educated are less dependent on ready access and a circle of acquaintances. Social, cultural, and economic context, therefore, greatly influence reading habits and interests. The respondents offered the following motives for reading: escape, pragmatic learning, cognitive order and information, personal meaning, reinforcement of beliefs, keeping up with the book talk of friends, and job or community position. In a larger survey, Ennis confirmed the relationship of education to amount of reading, finding that 20 percent of the readers accounted for 70 percent of the books read. The college educated read more, as did the more affluent.

Simpson, Ray H., and Anthony T. Soares. "Best and Least Liked Short Stories in Junior High School." *English Journal* 54 (February 1965), 108-111.
The study examines the responses of 4,250 students in grades seven to nine to 865 stories taken from anthologies. The students rated the stories on a 27-point scale from like to dislike. The stories consistently rated highest (20-24) and lowest (6-13) were analyzed according to a number of characteristics (five categories and 25 specific dimensions). The categories were mechanics of presentation, setting, characters, author and narrator, and plot and action. Students tended to prefer stories with more illustration and more space on the page, concrete language, more character descriptions and more main characters, less eminent authors, omniscient

narrator, a single strong unifying effect, more physical action, more conflict, more suspense, more dialogue, more concern with problems of the teenager. Setting, morality, satiric intent, and humorous quality were not significant.

Monson, Dianne L. "Children's Responses to Humorous Situations in Literature." Dissertation. University of Minnesota, 1966.
The study compared pupil responses to one unstructured versus three types of structured questions about humor in selected excerpts from children's literature. The researchers classified 580 fifth grade students by sex, reading level, socioeconomic level, and scholastic ability. Comparisons were made of responses to humor according to classification of humor: (1) character, (2) the unexpected, (3) the impossible, (4) author's use of words, and (5) a ridiculous situation. Structured questions, compared with unstructured questions, resulted in selections being considered more humorous for boys, for children in low socioeconomic groups, and for low and middle reading groups. Children in high intelligence groups judged excerpts humorous more often than did children in middle and low intelligence groups. In the groups studied, there were few differences in choices of categories of humor. There were no differences in responses of boys and girls. The results of the study indicated that there were differences in the way children of different intelligence, sex, socioeconomic level, and reading level groups respond to various forms of questioning about literature.

Shirley, Fehl L. "The Influence of Reading on Concepts, Attitudes, and Behavior." Dissertation. University of Arizona, Phoenix, 1966.
The study explored the effects of reading on the developing of self-images or self-concepts in adolescents. Four hundred and seventy students were asked to tell how specific books influenced them. Correlations were made between reported influence, age, intelligence, vocabulary, and grade level. Case studies of five highly in-

fluenced and five poorly influenced students were undertaken. The students' responses were classified into seven areas: self-image, philosophy of life, awareness of cultural groups, awareness of social problems, sensitivity to people, political influences, and miscellaneous. The responses were also categorized by degree: the indifferent, the observer, the participator, the synthesizer of constructs, and the decision maker. Some of the findings were these: 13 percent of the students reacted as construct synthesizers and 11 percent as self-image synthesizers; of the influences reported, 45 percent were on concepts, 40 percent on attitudes, 15 percent on behavior; a positive relationship existed between influences reported and intelligence, vocabulary, and comprehension; a negative relationship, between influences reported and age and grade level.

Purves, Alan C., and Victoria Rippere. *Elements of Writing about a Literary Work: A Study of Response to Literature.* NCTE Research Report, no. 9. Urbana, Illinois: National Council of Teachers of English, 1968.

The authors set forth a means of analyzing the content of written and oral responses to a work of literature, so that the responses of individuals may be compared in a neutral and descriptive fashion. There are four categories describing the posture of the person writing about literature: he describes his state of involvement in the literary work, his perception of that work—either analytic or classificatory—his interpretation of the meaning or significance of the work or a part of the work, and his evaluation of the work. Under these four categories, and a fifth, or miscellaneous, category for statements found in essays on a literary work but not dealing directly with that work, fall some 120 elements. Between the generality of the four categories and the specificity of the elements lie 23 subcategories:

1. Engagement-Involvement: engagement general, reaction to literature, reaction to form, reaction to content

2. Perception: perception general, language, literary devices, content, relation of technique to content, structure, tone, literary classification, contextual classification
3. Interpretation: interpretation general, interpretation of style, interpretation of content, mimetic interpretation, typological interpretation, hortatory interpretation
4. Evaluation: evaluation general, affective evaluation, evaluation of method, evaluation of author's vision

There are two major ways of reporting the patterns of response of a given population. The first is to take the essay as the unit and to determine the mean percent of statements devoted to each category, subcategory, or element. From the means, one may draw a profile of a group and compare that profile with the profile of another group. A second way of reporting is to postulate a number of paradigm essays and compare the populations with the paradigm. The paradigm would start with the element which defines the thesis of an essay and would follow with those elements which one would expect would support it. Ten sample paradigms are discussed.

There is an appendix, "The Practical Reader," in which are elaborated the ways by which one can mark a written response into statements and code them. It gives examples of those problematic statements which seem to fall into two classifications, and it gives four sample essays about a fictitious story and their analyses according to the elements.

Studies Related to the Teaching of Literature

Coryell, Nancy G. "An Evaluation of Extensive and Intensive Teaching of Literature. A Year's Experiment in the Eleventh Grade." *Teachers College Contributions to Education,* no. 175. New York: Bureau of Publications, Teachers College, Columbia University, 1927.
Coryell compared the results of teaching many works and treating

each rapidly and of teaching a few works which were analyzed in a detailed fashion. The pupils were divided into seven groups, one control and six experimental, according to whether the teaching was extensive or intensive and whether the pupils were superior, average, or low in verbal and reading ability. The groups were controlled for teacher effect. The treatment lasted a year and was measured by an examination of discussion, by six tests on commonly taught works (the tests spaced throughout the year), and by external measures of reading, literature, appreciation, and taste. The two groups scored equally well on the measures, and no clear pattern of the superiority of any one appeared. Some differences between ability groups emerged. The stenographic reports showed distinct differences in type, the extensive group discussing questions considered of high value and concentrating their discussion on fewer question types. The students also talked more in the extensive-teaching classes, and they preferred those classes.

Kangley, Lucy. "Poetry Preferences in the Junior High School." *Teachers College Contributions to Education,* no. 758. New York: Bureau of Publications, Teachers College, Columbia University, 1938.

This study tested the appeal of contrasting types of poetry. Poems were categorized as follows: (1) simple descriptive images or involved imagery; (2) obvious sound effects (repetition, onomatopoeia) or subtle sound effects (variation of meter); (3) human interest in nature or no human interest; (4) implied ethical lesson or direct ethical lesson; (5) commonplace subject matter or romantic subject matter; (6) comic and absurd humor or whimsical and ironic humor.

Selections by 355 eighth graders from paired-comparison poems showed that poems in the first category were preferred. Characteristics ranking high were obvious sound effects, commonplace subject matter, and obvious humor, while straight didactic matter, complex imagery, and nonhuman nature ranked low. Students with high reading comprehension scores favored the second category poems while students with low reading comprehension scores preferred obvious sound effects and obvious humor. Reasons for preferences were (in order): humor, marked rhythm, imagery, ethical purpose, and realism. Students often could not explain their reasons for their preferences.

LaBrant, Lou L., and Frieda M. Heller. "An Evaluation of Free Reading in Grades Seven to Twelve Inclusive." *Contributions in Education*, no. 4. Columbus, Ohio: Ohio State University Press, 1939; and

LaBrant, Lou L. "The Use of Communication Media." In *The Guinea Pigs after Twenty Years*, edited by Margaret Willis, pp. 127-164. Columbus, Ohio: Ohio State University, 1961.

This study traced the reading interests of one class through seventh, eighth, and ninth grades (1932-35) and another class through tenth, eleventh, and twelfth grades (1932-35), both of which participated in an experimental free-reading program. Self-selection of books was encouraged on the basis of students' needs. Students kept reading records, and selections were categorized by types.

From grades seven to nine, students' amount, variety, and sophistication of reading increased. Fiction was preferred overall; boys preferred nonfiction. An increase in reading of nonfiction, adult fiction, and drama and a decreased interest in "series" books was found. From grades ten to twelve, an increase in reading of drama, poetry, American writers, and more contemporary writers and a decrease in narrative-fiction was found.

A follow-up study in 1955 of 42 of the 54 students in the grades seven to nine study (who comprised 80 percent of the graduating class of 1938) found that the amount of these adults' reading markedly exceeded that of comparable groups reported in other studies, that the women read three times as many books as men, that men nonreaders outnumbered women nonreaders, that college had a negative influence on the reading habits of many, and that the books read were more sophisticated than those read by the general public.

Vergara, Allys D. "A Critical Study of a Group of College Women's Responses to Poetry." *Teachers College Contributions to Education,* no. 923. New York: Bureau of Publications, Teachers College, Columbia University, 1946.
The study investigated the variations in comprehension of poetry among college students by securing free responses from a small group, more controlled responses from a larger group, and scores on an objective test from a still larger group, the responses to be checked against intelligence and literary tests. Vergara analyzed the leisurely response of five women to 64 poems. The women were asked only to consider the sense and mood of the poems, discussing them individually as they perceived imagistic, symbolistic, tone color, and rhythmic poems (the four distinctions referring to emphasis rather than school). Vergara notes the relation of background to response, compares the responses to poems read silently and those read orally, and finds a general importance of theme rather than aesthetic quality. The second group of 15 students read 48 poems less leisurely and wrote four-sentence responses describing sense and mood. A time restriction was placed on the responses. These were also analyzed, and the finding was that background, especially a background in the arts, was a stronger factor in correct response than was intelligence. The oral method seemed to be more effective with the less able students. The third group consisted of two populations of 28, one that heard the poems and one that read them, both being asked objective questions. No significant differences between treatments were found, and the test proved unreliable. A supplementary study using the Hartley test found the oral group superior.

Norvell, George W. *The Reading Interests of Young People.* Boston, Massachusetts: D. C. Heath and Company, 1950.

This study analyzed preferences of 50 thousand students, grades seven through twelve, based on preference ratings of each title studied or read by the students during a school year. Rating scores were correlated with a number of variables, and interest type categories were derived. Interest scores were closer to the true scores for children in general if the data was from several teachers' classes rather than one, from several schools rather than one school. Students of high, average, and low intelligence and reading ability had similar interests. The average rate of change in preference between grades varied considerably due to individual differences. The divergence in ages among students of the same grade was not a significant factor in preferences for that grade. Selections which are primarily reflective, philosophic, religious, or artistic (as opposed to dramatic) rated higher in the eleventh grade than in the eighth grade. Sex was a highly significant factor, girls preferring seven of the literary types more than boys. Boys preferred adventure, sports, school life, mystery, obvious humor, and animals, but disliked love, sentiments, family life, didacticism, religion, extended description, female characters, and form or technique as a dominant factor. Girls' preferences were similar except for more interest in school life, sentiments, and love and less interest in grim adventure. Comparison of 24 "free-reading" classes with 24 traditional classes found small but significant gains in reading comprehension for the "free-reading" approach; the vast majority of teachers and students favored this approach.

Gray, William S., and Bernice Rogers. *Maturity in Reading: Its Nature and Appraisal.* Chicago, Illinois: University of Chicago Press, 1956.
This study examined the nature and extent of the reading of adults divided by level of education. Three groups—with eighth grade, with some high school, and with more than high school education—were studied intensively (the total number of subjects was 38). The subjects responded to scaled questions dealing with eighteen aspects of

reading (e.g., interest, purposes, nature of material, understanding, reactions, and transfer of reading to other aspects of life). In general all the subjects scored below the midpoint of the scales and significantly below nine other readers selected as "well-read, superior readers." The low and the middle groups ranked below the higher on maturity scales, but equally on interest in reading, purposes of reading, and materials read. There were differences in competence. Other findings include these: interest and purpose for reading are not closely related to school training, although competence is; a person's activities, not his needs, determine the maturity of his reading interests and purposes; competence in reading sets bounds to the amount of reading, but the relationship between the two is complex in that the competent reader may not read widely (something else seems to have happened in his education). Gray and Rogers followed this study with a series of interviews with well-read adults to derive a second set of scales. These showed that reading seemed to follow a specific interest, usually an interest outside of the sphere of job or home. The main factors influencing reading seemed to be the cultural influence of the home, past pleasant experiences with reading, and some instruction in the values of reading.

Lehtovaara, A., and P. Saarinen. *School-Age Reading Interests: A Methodological Approach.* Helsinki, Finland: Suomalainen Tiedeakatemia, 1964.
This study investigated four methods of measuring reading interests: the questionnaire using a list of book types, the booklist using actual titles and short descriptions, the text sample, and the paired comparison. Each of these methods was tried with children aged 10 and 15, for whom information about reading habits and library use was also obtained. Parallel questionnaires, each with 26 types of books, were developed, and the students were asked to rate each type on a five point scale. The paired-comparison method used the book types, combining some of those types that seemed similar into 14 categories or 91 comparisons. Each student was given one of the

four forms at six-week intervals. In general the strongly positive and strongly negative choices remained consistent across forms, but the correlations between test types averaged about .50. The methods were then compared as they indicated changes in reading interests between the two age groups. The book list and text samples agreed with each other best, perhaps because of the similarity in source. The paired comparisons yielded markedly different results, perhaps because of the difference in test format. The differences between methods were more apparent with the younger group than with the older and with boys than with girls. The changes in actual preference were similar to those found in other surveys, although the differences between students in elementary schools and those in selective schools were significant, as were those between boys and girls. A factor analysis was performed on the questionnaires: for the ten year olds the main factors were adventure, girls' stories, adult books, descriptive or narrative style, and knowledge; for the 14 and 15 year olds, the factors were adventure, girls' stories, love stories, symbolic-aesthetic elements, descriptive or narrative style, and knowledge.

Steinberg, Erwin R., et al. *A Senior High School Curriculum in English for Able College-Bound Students.* Pittsburgh, Pennsylvania: Carnegie Institute of Technology, 1965.
This study evaluated a curriculum for grades ten through twelve, the literature component of which moved from thematic concerns to aesthetic and formal ones. The researchers developed a literary discernment test, a multiple-choice test on a short story, covering the categories of understanding those features of a story which make it entertaining, of understanding the craft of the writer, and of understanding the plot and theme of the story. On the same story was a literary preference questionnaire, which asked the student to choose among comments on the story. The comments were coded: facts about the work or writer, entertaining features, craft of the writer, and plot and theme. The last two were considered more de-

sirable options. In addition there was an attitude questionnaire using the semantic differential about concepts of literature and a free interpretation of a story. Comparisons with a control group showed that the experimental group was superior on the literary discernment test at all grade levels. Other results were indeterminate.

McNeil, Elton B. "Hooked on Research." In *Hooked on Books: Program and Proof*, by D. Fader and E. B. McNeil, pp. 180-226. New York: Berkeley Publishing Corporation, 1966.

This study seeks to evaluate the "English in Every Classroom" curriculum project sponsored by Program English of the United States Office of Education, a project designed to test free reading and free writing for disadvantaged youth. Using two groups of adolescent boys in training schools, a control group of 31, and an experimental group of 60, testing was conducted over a period of two years. The several measures are perhaps the most significant aspect of the study: a teacher's behavior rating sheet to discover teacher perceptions of the students as "good" or "bad"; a teacher's evaluation form to arrive at estimates of the pupil's sense of self-worth, attention span, reaction to failure, and relationship with others; a "How Much Do You Like" form about student attitudes toward activities; a behavioral rating form to measure student self-perception, e.g., as school lover or school hater; a "How Do You Feel about Things in Class" form to learn attitudes toward school (e.g., anxiety and need for achievement); a literary attitude scale, a semantic differential; and a verbal proficiency test. Significant differences were found in favor of the experimental group on the following scales: teacher sense of self-worth, behavioral rating form, literary attitude scale, "How Do You Feel about Things in Class" scale, and the *Stanford Achievement Test*. Results also showed that in both groups white students achieved significantly better scores than black students. The study is important primarily for its development of attitude and other affective measures.

Nelms, Ben F. "Characteristics of Poetry Associated with Preferences of a Panel of Tenth Grade Students." Dissertation. University of Iowa, Iowa City, 1967.

For this study, 100 poems were selected at random from literature textbooks and poetry anthologies appropriate for tenth graders, and another 20 poems were selected from three anthologies of modern poems. Sixteen "representative" tenth grade students from the university high school rated each of the poems on 29 semantic differential scales after hearing each poem read by the same person on tape (the students held copies of the poems). The poems were presented in ten different sessions, 12 poems per session. A panel of seven sophisticated readers of poetry then reacted to each of the poems on ten scales reflecting characteristics of poetry. The poems were also classified according to topical content by experienced English teachers. Multiple regression analysis showed that the students tended to prefer poems with narrative interest; that the subject matter of the poems, more than the form or style, affected their preferences; that clarity and comprehension increased their preference for a poem; that regular rhyming schemes and strong rhythmic patterns had little influence on preferences; that the students tended to prefer good modern poems over British and American "classics"; and that the quality of the poems had little relation to the students' preferences. The students also had low interest in the brief lyric expression of emotions, moods, or sensory impressions but responded to the development of a narrative or thematic climax, the cataloging of sensory impressions, and the use of a light satiric tone.

Shnayer, Sidney W. "Some Relationships between Reading Interest and Reading Comprehension." Dissertation. University of California at Berkeley, 1967.

The study examined the responses of 578 sixth grade students in order to determine the relationships between levels of interest and the comprehension of material. Students were given social scale tests and intelligence tests and were divided into groups on the basis of reading comprehension tests. Each group was required to read 15 stories with readability scores two grades higher than the mean reading ability of the group, rate each story on a four-point scale, and answer questions of fact, sequence, and inference about each one. The results were examined first for the interrelation of reading interest and comprehension, and it was found that the difference between groups was highly significant regardless of the interest. Boys' comprehension was lower than that of girls, although the reverse was true for three subgroups. The comprehension of high interest and low interest stories within a group also differed significantly (P = .001). Further, the comprehension scores did vary as a function of both the ability of the reading group and the level of interest in stories read. The effect of interest diminishes as ability increases. Further, low interest functions to differentiate between reading groups, but not high interest, so that the cumulative effect of little or no interest becomes increasingly important.

Burton, Dwight, et al. *The Development and Testing of Approaches to the Teaching of English in the Junior High School.* Final Report, USOE Project No. H-026. Tallahassee, Florida: Florida State University, 1968.
The study tested the effectiveness of three curricular approaches: the tripod approach of literature, language, and composition; the theme-centered approach, and the cognitive-processes approach. Each approach was tried in two junior high schools for three years and the students were given common measures at the end of the ninth grade. In literature, the measures included objective tests of the ability to read poetry and prose, a semantic differential, and free responses to prose and poetry analyzed according to the schema developed by Squire. The findings showed no significant differences between the curricula—the teachers accounted for most of the variance. There were differences in the type of response: students in the tripod approach made more literary responses; students in the

theme approach, more interpretational responses. The study suggests the centrality of the teacher variable.

Gallo, Donald R. "The Construction and Validation of an Instrument to Assess Teachers' Opinions of Methods of Teaching Poetry to Tenth Grade Students of Average Ability." Dissertation. Syracuse University, 1968.

The purpose of this study was to construct an instrument for assessing teachers' opinions of methods of teaching poetry to average ability tenth grade students and to validate the instrument by determining the relationship between scores on the *Poetry Methods Rating Scale* and teachers' attitudes, personality, performance, and success in the classroom. The final 38-item-scale and a scoring key were formed from the responses of 32 experts in English education. Thirty-nine tenth grade teachers from 14 schools took the *Poetry Methods Rating Scale*, the *Minnesota Teacher Attitude Inventory*, the *Teaching Situation Reaction Test*, and the *Rokeach Dogmatism Scale*. On the basis of their scores on the *Poetry Methods Rating Scale*, 25 teachers were randomly selected to teach three short poems to one of their classes. A committee of 3 judges then evaluated each of the lessons which the teachers had recorded on audio tape, and each class took a multiple-choice test on the three poems. The fourteen teachers who did not teach the poems were asked to administer the poetry test to one of their classes as a control group. As a further evaluation of effective teaching, all of the students in the classes that had studied the poems were asked to evaluate their teachers by means of a questionnaire.

A significant (.05) relationship was found between the *Poetry Methods Rating Scale* and the *Teaching Situation Reaction Test*, but there was no significant relationship with the *Minnesota Teacher Attitude Inventory* or the *Rokeach Dogmatism Scale*. A t-test of the difference between the means in these three comparisons resulted in a significant difference (.10 level) favoring teachers scoring above the mean on the *Poetry Methods Rating Scale* in students' evaluations of teachers. Teachers scoring above the mean on the *Poetry Methods Rating Scale* were more likely to be first year teachers or to have taught from six to ten years, to subscribe to more journals, and to have a master's degree. Also students of teachers scoring high on the *Poetry Methods Rating Scale* read more poetry and enjoyed studying the three poems more.

The investigator concluded that the *Poetry Methods Rating Scale* is a reliable instrument for assessing opinions of methods of teaching poetry, but that its validity is tenuous. Analysis of the tapes of teachers teaching poetry lessons caused the investigator to conclude that what teachers know and believe—or at least say they know and believe—about methods of teaching poetry does not always result in related behaviors in their classes.

Klein, Howard A. "Interest and Comprehension in Sex-Typed Materials." Dissertation. Syracuse University, 1968.
The study sought to determine how the occupation and sex of the main character in a story affect the interest and comprehension of fifth grade children. Using the semantic differential and the cloze test as measures, the study investigated 312 children in Canada. The stories were about ballet dancers, pilots, and social workers, each topic being told in a version with a male and with a female main character. The findings indicated that sex-appropriate occupations were rated higher in interest by each sex, that boys rated male characters higher in only the pilot story, but that girls rated the female character higher in each story. The reactions on the semantic differential showed the distinct male-female differences in pattern of response, but these patterns had only a mixed relation to the comprehension scores. Although the ratings of the pilot and the ballet dancer stories differed greatly, the mean scores for boys and girls were identical. The sex of the central character in a story seemed to have little relation to comprehension. Finally, there were differences between high and low scoring children: the higher scoring children were little affected by their preferences, the lower

scoring children performed better on the preferred sex-typed content.

Zais, Robert. "The Sophistication of Reading Interests as Related to Selected Personality Factors and Certain Other Characteristics of High School Students." Dissertation. University of Connecticut, Storrs, 1968.
The study reported the results of a scale especially constructed to measure the sophistication of reading interests by creating brief story synopses. The levels of sophistication run from interest in plot, physical conflict, and stereotyped characters, to interest in characters, psychological conflict, and generalized theme, to interest in idea and theme, psychological conflict, and symbolic characterization. The measure contained 13 types of stories—each with a synopsis written to satisfy each of the levels of sophistication—and was validated with a group of teachers. The final form of the test used an interlocking series of pairs of selections (not matched for subject), rather than triads. After reliability and validity checks, the measure was used to study the choices of students in grades nine through twelve. In combination, personality variables were not significantly related to sophistication of reading interests, but sex, age, IQ, and reading achievement were. Taken singly, benevolence, conformity (for the males), sex, IQ, and reading achievement were related to sophistication. None of the factors or combinations, however, was strongly enough correlated to warrant use as a predictor of sophistication.

Johns, Jerry L. "Expressed Reading Preferences of Intermediate-Grade Students in Urban Settings." Dissertation. Michigan State University, East Lansing, 1970.
This study investigated whether inner-city children in grades four, five, and six express a greater preference for stories or books dealing with inner-city life than for other topics. The study involved 599 students (515 of them black) and asked them to examine illus-

trations and descriptions from modern realistic fiction dealing with either the inner-city or suburbia. Each child responded to a brief questionnaire about each selection. The process was repeated with selections in which the variables were characters with positive and with negative self-concepts, and with selections in which the variable was positive and negative group interaction. The major findings showed that inner-city children expressed a statistically significant $(P = .01)$ preference for stories which depict middle-class settings, characters with positive self-concepts, and characters in positive group interactions. Other variables affecting preference included age for setting, grade and sex for group interactions, perception of home environment and setting, self-concept and character, and peer-group perception and group interaction. Intelligence and race did not contribute to the variance.

Hoetker, James. *Students as Audiences: An Experimental Study of the Relationships between Classroom Study of Drama and Attendance at the Theatre.* NCTE Research Report, no. 11. Urbana, Illinois: National Council of Teachers of English, 1971.
This study evaluated the predictions of English teachers and theatre people about the effects upon students of different ways of preparing them to attend professional productions of *Macbeth* and O'Casey's *Red Roses for Me.* The independent variables involved in the differing predictions were: timing of classroom treatment (before or after attending the play), contents of the lessons (the specific play being performed or a related one), the intensity of the study of the backgrounds (brief or intense), and the intensity of the study of the text of the play (brief or intense). The four two-level independent variables gave sixteen treatment conditions to be evaluated. The subjects were approximately 1,300 tenth grade students in the classes of 52 teachers, all of whom were participating in Rhode Island's Project Discovery. The experiment was so designed that any class's second play treatment was a mirror image of its first, so that each class acted as its own control group. A total of

13 pencil-and-paper tests in six broader categories were devised: affective response, knowledge, interpretive skills, philosophical insights, appreciation, and desirable attitudes and behaviors. Item sampling of these dependent measures made it possible to obtain large numbers of scores with a minimum of disruption of classes. Multivariate analysis of variance, with two covariates—verbal IQ and prior theatre experience—was used to evaluate the effects of the factors and their interactions upon all dependent measures simultaneously.

Significant effects were rather scarce, given the large number of hypotheses evaluated. Among the more interesting were these: the lowest scores on all knowledge tests were associated with the most intensive classroom treatments; higher knowledge test scores were associated with study prior to attendance at the play; higher scores on philosophical insights tests were associated with study of the specific play being performed and with specific study prior to the performance; the lowest appreciation test scores were associated with the most intensive classroom treatments.

Two general conclusions were reached. First, each group—teachers and actors—accurately predicted the direction of the effects of the different treatment conditions upon those outcomes they most highly valued. (An earlier study had established the objectives most highly valued by each group.) That is, the actors had advocated the combination of treatment variables that maximized appreciation; the teachers had advocated the combination of variables that maximized cognitive understandings. Second, both groups overestimated the size of the effects that could be produced by the manipulation of treatment conditions. Alternatively, the playgoing experience itself was so powerful a determinant of student responses that additional manipulations could rarely distinguish between groups with the playgoing experience in common.